Spiritual Truths for Rebuilding &
Revitalizing Your Marriage

From
ASHES *to*
BEAUTY

JEFF COLÓN

STUDY GUIDE INCLUDED

From ASHES *to* BEAUTY

JEFF COLÓN

www.purelifeministries.org

888.PURELIFE

*What others are saying about...*FROM ASHES TO BEAUTY

"Jeff Colón is on the front lines fighting the real-world battles the rest of us are either too scared to tackle or simply hoping someone else will rise up to engage. This man knows his stuff, and in the arenas of sexuality and marriage, this guy has earned his stripes. He's deserving of medals for his work with the sexually addicted and his wisdom in the arena of rescuing marriages under siege, is time tested and God-approved. Jeff is the guy you want in the foxhole with you – he's got a forehead of flint and a heart of gold."

ERIC LUDY,
Bestselling Author of *When God Writes Your Love Story*

"Jeff Colón has written a compelling and biblically powerful book that would give hope to any couple whose marriage is in trouble due to sexual sin. His message is Christ-centered. His humility is obviously God-given. His gratitude to the Lord overflows. His love for his wife that God has placed in his heart is clearly shown. I highly recommend this book for any couple struggling with a difficult marriage whether the difficulty is due to sexual sin or other sins. God will use Jeff's message to convict and to help you."

MARTHA PEACE,
Biblical Counselor and author of *The Excellent Wife*

"I am so thankful that Jeff Colón has written the book *From Ashes to Beauty* to help devastated couples rebuild their broken marriages! This will be a powerful resource for every pastor and every counselor trying to help couples rebuild their marriages after an affair.

Jeff speaks from personal experience about the incredible pain and destruction caused by the insidious lure of pornography and other sexual immorality. In his own gentle way, Jeff helps the reader to see that God can restore *any* marriage when both husband and wife learn and obey the Biblical principles of the daily walk with Christ. There is no shortcut, for as Jeff writes, "Only a deep relationship with Jesus Christ can produce a fulfilling marriage."

I have been blessed to know Jeff and Rose Colón personally and I'm convinced that you, too, will be blessed and given new hope that your marriage can be redeemed from the ashes of defeat. Read this book slowly and carefully, digesting each principle while you ask the Lord to change *your* heart. As Jeff points out, "God resists the proud, but gives grace to the humble." Through brokenness, humility, repentance, and obedience to God's Word, both husband and wife will experience a rebirth of hope and joy, and your marriage can become a beautiful experience that lasts a lifetime."

DR. ED BULKLEY,
President, *International Association of Biblical Counselors*
Pastor, *LIFE Fellowship*

*What others are saying about...*FROM ASHES TO BEAUTY

"In this most valuable work, Jeff Colón walks the reader without fear through the central issue of marital strife: hearts estranged from God. The content is refreshingly wise with biblical insight, readable and creative in helping marriages of any length rally at the foot of the cross, the true place of new beginnings. I highly recommend it.

DR. BILL HINES,
Author of *Leaving Yesterday Behind*
Dean of Biblical Counseling Dept.,
Masters International School of Divinity

"If you're looking for a marriage book that is more than just a re-hash of the same tired topics then this is it! Jeff and Rose Colón have dug below the surface of marriage struggles and have gone after the heart. Along the way they've also humbled themselves and allowed us to peek into the struggles of their own marriage journey, as well as displaying the incredible mercy and grace that God has poured out on them. Pastors and biblical counselors will be turning to this book again and again as they try to help couples truly repent and change, for the glory of God."

BRAD BIGNEY,
Senior Pastor, *Grace Fellowship Church*

"In his book, *From Ashes to Beauty*, Jeff Colón gives hope for couples who want to renew or restore their marriage. Whether your marriage is at a breaking point or if you want to simply improve it, the truths in this book will help you understand how the power of God can work in your own circumstances if you are willing to take God's way. Jeff explains how the Beatitudes can be lived out today practically by his personal testimony and the testimonies of others, showing how the work of the Holy Spirit can change your life and situation as you embrace the Cross. This book is written for those who will not be satisfied with a temporary fix, but truly want a changed life."

RUTH RUIBAL, D. Min.,
President; *Julio C. Ruibal Ministries*

"The truths from the Beatitudes revealed in *From Ashes to Beauty* will transform countless marriages when each spouse applies them to their life. We can think of no better time, than such a time as this, to publish this anointed work. So many marriages have been ravaged and torn apart by sexual sin. In his writing, Jeff reveals the inner healing of his own fragmented marriage and the miraculous transformation as Christ put each piece back together. We applaud Jeff and Rose as heroes in the battle to set the captives free."

BOBBY & DIANNE LLOYD,
Founders, *Clean Hands & Pure Heart*
Long Island, New York

*What others are saying about...*FROM ASHES TO BEAUTY

"In the midst of an ungodly society with the moral fabric of the American family fading away, Jeff Colón, in his book *From Ashes to Beauty*, has captured the golden Biblical truths for the institution of Marriage whereby the "two shall become one." I've had the privilege of being a part of Jeff and Rose Colón's redemption journey and have been truly blessed to see Jeff literally become transformed from the "ash heap to the beauty of holiness." Their miracle testimony continues to inspire and transform everyone they encounter, through Pure Life Ministries and conferences around the world. The transparency of Jeff's testimony along with the others in each chapter is compelling and life changing. I'm so thankful that Jeff and Rose have unveiled their life story, that all who read this book may too capture God's golden Biblical truths for their marriage and the family."

JIMMY JACK,
Executive Director and Pastor of *Freedom Chapel*,
Metro New York Teen Challenge

"I have counseled married couples for over 13,000 hours in the past 35 years, as a pastor and minister, and have over 1,500 books in my personal library on marriage and relationships - so I read the manuscript of Jeff Colón's new book on marriage, avidly. Jeff's book, *From Ashes to Beauty*, will help every married couple. It's scriptural, personal, and filled with powerful examples drawn from real life. I highly recommend, *From Ashes to Beauty*. It's probably the most honest book on the struggles of marriage that I have ever read. What is unique about Jeff's book is his reliance on the Holy Spirit in his struggle to rebuild his marriage. The Scriptures that Jeff uses and applies to marriage - alone - would be worth the price of the book. Jeff Colón is also an anointed minister, counselor, preacher, teacher - and my highest praise - a real man of God. *From Ashes to Beauty*, by Jeff Colón, is a "must have" book on marriage and relationships, for every married couple, pastor, and counselor! As I read, *From Ashes to Beauty*, the thing that stood out to me as the most helpful aspect of the book was the amazing wealth of material to help couples resolve conflict in their marriage. "GET IT NOW!"

RANDY JONES,
Pastor of *Christ Our Lord Church*,
President of *Word of Truth Ministries*,
former Director of Evangelism and Off-Campus Dean,
Christ for the Nations, Dallas, Texas

DEDICATION

I dedicate this book to my wife Rose,
who loved me and prayed for me when there was
no light at the end of the tunnel.

ACKNOWLEDGMENTS

I want to especially thank Ed Buch for laboring in love for many months to organize, refine and edit my thoughts into a cohesive manuscript.

Thanks also to Gary Meeks and TJ McAuley for their contributions, as well as to the counseling staff at Pure Life Ministries for their help in creating the study guide.

ALSO AVAILABLE FROM PURE LIFE MINISTRIES:

At the Altar of Sexual Idolatry
A Biblical Guide to Counseling the Sexual Addict
Create in Me a Pure Heart
How America Lost Her Innocence
He Leads Me Beside Still Waters
Intoxicated with Babylon
Irresistible to God
A Lamp Unto My Feet
Living in Victory
Out of the Depths of Sexual Sin
Pressing On Toward the Heavenly Calling
Standing Firm through the Great Apostasy
The Walk of Repentance

For these books and other resources please contact:

PURE LIFE MINISTRIES
14 School Street
Dry Ridge, KY 41035
(888) PURELIFE - to order
(859) 813-0005 FAX
www.purelifeministries.org

FROM ASHES TO BEAUTY

ISBN 0-9800286-1-2
EAN 978-0-9800286-1-4

CONTENTS

$\mathscr{F}$OREWORD

$\mathscr{R}$ecently a friend of mine confided to me that he had been struggling with a particular type of habitual sin. Although he was very hesitant to bring his secret life into the light, desperation finally drove him to seek help. It was then that he found the healing and forgiveness he had been longing for.

You've got to know that it was a very humbling moment for him to walk through those doors the first time. "What would someone think if they saw me there?" he worried. "What if my friends and family found out?" He, like most men, felt that he could fix any problem that might come his way by himself. When he had to ask others for help, he was admitting that he was in trouble…that he was weak. This is not something that most men would readily say.

So what was the result of him taking that first humbling step? In a word…*strength*. Yes, strength comes from humbling moments. There's an old adage that says: "That which doesn't kill us makes us stronger." Well, I suppose there's some truth to that, but it's not from the Bible. What Scripture *does* say is that God gives strength to the humble. (I Peter 5:5-6)

If you are thinking, "My marriage can never again be beautiful because I have destroyed it with my sexual sin;" or if you feel as weak and defeated as you ever have; or if you have resigned yourself to the thought that your situation is too far gone and beyond hope; please hear me. Amazing strength is being offered to you and your spouse—yes, it is strength that is beyond you—but nevertheless it is being made available to you!

There are four "miracle marriage" true stories described in this book. The names are *Danny and Paula, Tom and Sue, Bill and Teri,* and *Carl and Linda.* They were just four normal American couples. To the outside observer they probably would have looked like happy Christian marriages. But when sexual sin entered in, each one of these marriages was nearly destroyed.

Well… allow me to add "miracle marriage number five" to the list. Their names: *Clay and Renee.* That's right, my wife and I have walked a road of healing very similar to the couples in this book. In 1998, I confessed to Renee that I was viewing pornography. I had gotten to the point that I was sick of it. Actually, the truth is that I was sick of me. Although I never actually committed adultery, in my mind I had many times.

That humbling moment when I confessed this to Renee has opened up our marriage to blessings that we never had experienced beforehand. I know that confession can be very painful; it sure was for me! But in some supernatural—only by God—way, He provided us with the strength to endure the healing process we went through over the months and years that followed. Today, we can truly say that we are thankful for that season because of where He has brought us!

I encourage you not to resist God's dealings with you. Admit what you've done, repent of your sins and run to Jesus like never before!

With this book, Jeff Colón offers you a solid and biblical approach to deal with the issues you will face as a couple. He uses the Beatitudes from Matthew 5 to guide you and your spouse into healing, hope and ultimately into victory! You may look at that word *victory* and still see no way that you and your spouse could ever get there. You may think, "That's great for those couples in the book, but my marriage is just over, there's simply no going back."

I'll say it again: Run to Jesus like never before! He loves you both more than you know and He wants to perform His marvelous work in your marriage. Do you think this task is beyond Him? Think again. He is supremely able, and lovingly willing, to walk with you and provide the strength that is seemingly beyond you.

Clay Crosse
holyhomes.org

ℐNTRODUCTION

*T*he burden in my heart had been constantly growing. While counseling couples over the years and seeing firsthand the devastation wrought by sexual sin upon so many marriages, the grief mounted to the point where I felt compelled to do more. I was especially grieved to see so many marriages being relegated to the ash heap of divorce. This book was birthed out of that burden of grief and the conviction that things do not have to be this way, especially among Christians.

I know in my heart that no situation is beyond God's ability to restore. Since God restored my marriage with Rose 15 years ago, I have witnessed countless marriages reclaimed from the ash heap and transformed into beautiful representations of God's love and forgiveness. That's what can happen when true repentance occurs and each spouse enters into vital contact with God, His great, precious promises, and His will for their lives. God does not change; He still gives us beauty for ashes. (Isaiah 61:3)

The spiritual truths shared in this book are designed to bring about a deeper walk with God for both spouses. That is the answer to your situation, whatever it may be. You will find that as you draw close to God He takes care of the problems that seem so big to us. *There is absolutely no reason why a truly "Christian" marriage should ever fail, even after sexual sin has occurred.* When both spouses are living in a vital and intimate relationship with Jesus, everything else will follow.

Fifteen years ago, as Rose and I surveyed the effects of sexual sin on our marriage, all we saw was a mountainous pile of rubble and ashes. We empathized with Nehemiah and how he must have felt when he received the report of Jerusalem's condition: "The survivors who are left from the captivity in the province are there in *great distress* and reproach. The wall of Jerusalem is also *broken* down, and its gates are *burned* with fire." Nehemiah had the overwhelming task before him of having to rebuild the walls from this state of utter ruin. He knew that his only source of strength and hope must come from the One who could do what was impossible for man. Consequently, he tearfully prayed for God to intervene: "So it was, when I heard these words that I sat down and wept, and mourned for many days; I was fasting and praying before the God of heaven." (Nehemiah 1:3-4, emphasis added)

Like Nehemiah witnessing the devastation of sin and its consequences, a couple dealing with the aftermath of sexual sin faces the same overwhelming sense of destruction and despair over what lies ahead. All they can see is the huge pile of debris remaining from what used to be their marriage. Shattered emotionally, they are easily overwhelmed. Battered spiritually, they are rife with uncertainty. Restoring and rebuilding their marriage is a daunting task. Like Nehemiah, their only source of strength and hope must come from the One who can do what is impossible for man.

Beloved, allow God to draw you to Him through these pages and He will turn your mountainous issues into mole hills and give you more than you bargained for. Don't limit God, He has so much He wants to give you and your spouse in every situation and through every trial you will face.

I assure you, God can give you the spiritual wherewithal to rebuild your marriage out of the ruins of sexual sin, or any kind of difficulty that may have arisen in your marriage. As you go through this book, please do so prayerfully and remain open to what God has for you. Take your time and don't be in a hurry; God isn't in a hurry. You may even want to go over some things more than once. At the back of the book you will find a study guide for each chapter. I have included this to help you apply what you have read and to allow God to do for you spiritually what He wants to do. The Word of God tells us that being hearers only is not profitable. (James 1:22) These assignments should be done with that in mind. God has something for you, but you will have to do what He is asking.

*"I, Jeff, take thee, Rose to be
my wedded wife, to have and to hold
from this day forward, for better, for worse,
for richer, for poorer, in sickness or in health,
to love and to cherish, 'til death do us part,
according to God's holy ordinance;
thereto I pledge my love."*

Chapter One

PREREQUISITES TO A RESTORED MARRIAGE

*I*t was May 4, 1991. The sky was painted a heavenly blue and accented with lazy white clouds. The early spring foliage was a rich green, and even the air seemed fresh and clean in New York City that morning. It was the beautiful, pristine kind of day couples dream about for their marriage ceremony. Rose, my wife to be, stood hand in hand with me at the altar. As we expressed our wedding vows to one another, I looked into her eyes and I could see the same bright hopefulness and expectation that every bride has on her wedding day.

Her hopes were anchored in the belief that I would love and cherish her and meet her needs. She had expectations that I would provide and care for her, and give her a life of happiness with abundant blessings. Isn't that what we all expect from our marriage? Isn't our mate supposed to complete and fulfill us, and to make all of our dreams come true? Isn't that how all of the storybook romances end, and shouldn't we, too, expect to live happily ever after?

Nevertheless, it only took a few weeks before our fairy tale crumbled as my twelve-year history of sexual sin and drug abuse resurfaced. Rose was devastated. Here we were, just three months into our marriage, and I was off to a Christian drug rehab program. I spent the next eight months away from home, but we clung to the hope that our marriage would be better when I got out.

During my time in rehab, the Lord gave my wife a Scripture that helped her to hold on: "Do not fear, for you will not be ashamed; nor be disgraced, for you will not be put to shame; for you will forget the shame of your youth...For your Maker is your Husband...the Lord has called you like a woman forsaken and grieved in spirit, like a youthful wife when you were refused." (Isaiah 54:4-6) Although Rose may not have fully understood at this point, the Lord was revealing to her that it was *His will* for her to pass through this barren wilderness, where there would be many tears. She was confident that He had called her to this but desperately hung on to the hope that she would soon "forget the shame of her youth." She latched onto the encouraging aspect of this word from God, thinking to herself, "Finally, I will have a wonderful marriage. Things will be different; now we can enjoy a happy life together."

Little did we know, the worst had just begun, and we had only started our long, hard journey.

Two weeks after I completed Teen Challenge, I was back to my old ways. I resumed my pursuit of sin, sometimes spending days away from home living in seedy motels. I had encounters with prostitutes in my hotel room or in my car right on the street. I watched pornography for hours at a time while getting high on crack cocaine. After each binge, I returned home to Rose, earnestly vowing never to do it again. I faithfully attended church and dutifully "repented" at the altar following each binge. Afterward, I would do well for a short time, only to fall back into the same pattern every few months. Each time I failed, Rose felt greater despair and hopelessness. "Is this all I have to look forward to?" she would ask herself. "Is this the way marriage is supposed to be? What's wrong with *ME?* Why am I not enough for him? Why is God punishing me like this? I thought I married a godly man...he's part of the worship team in our church every Sunday. *Where is God in all of this?*"

After pursuing my sin over and over again, my pastor, Jimmy Jack, finally intervened. He recommended that I enter a program under the auspices of Times Square Church in Manhattan called Timothy House. I spent *another* three months away from home. In spite of all I was putting her through, Rose would faithfully drive into the seedy neighborhood where I was staying to visit me every week. Something seemed to be happening in me and she valiantly held onto the marriage with all the hope she could muster.

We both felt that our lives would be different when I left the program. And I was different—for a while. The confidence I felt in dealing with my addictions grew, and the outward results were positive. Several months of "sobriety" buoyed Rose's hopes. We were both in for yet another bitter disappointment, though. It wasn't long before I returned to the pig pen, wallowing in the muck and mire of my sin and dragging our marriage vows back through the cesspool. I came to realize later that the success I initially enjoyed during that time came from my own determination—a faulty foundation built on the sinking sand of self-reliance.

Despite the intervention of two good Christian programs, the end result left Rose living with a Dr. Jekyll and Mr. Hyde. From Sunday to Friday, I played the part of a Christian, one who could easily talk the talk when necessary, and worked at my job as an elevator mechanic in Manhattan. But by Friday something would begin to come over me, and I would inevitably spend the next 36 hours in the filthy world of 42nd Street visiting adult bookstores, smoking crack cocaine and hooking up with prostitutes. Nevertheless, Sunday morning I would be right back in church playing in the worship team as if nothing had happened. The future of our marriage seemed bleak to Rose and yet, she felt as though the Lord wanted her to stick it out. I felt just as hopeless: nothing is more miserable than knowing the truth while living in unrepentant sin.

Like most men who are living in habitual sin, I was a master at deception. I had all the right lines for my wife whenever questionable things came up. Later, when the truth came out, she was left with the same old feelings of betrayal. She was constantly made to feel like the fool, trying to believe her husband even when her intuition told her differently.

Rose didn't always know how to respond. Sometimes she would even explode in anger. One time I came home and found all of my belongings strewn all over the street, thrown out the window from our fifth floor apartment. Of course, there were also plenty of moments when she felt as though she just couldn't endure another disappointment and that it was time to leave. Inevitably though, the Lord would move on her heart and she would once again forgive me and encourage me to get right with God. Sometimes she would even pray all night for me while I was out carousing. Meanwhile, I continued to trample on her heart, leaving her in a long, dark tunnel with no light at the end.

After three years of marriage, my dual role as a "Christian" husband and a drug-using sex addict came crashing down. My life was a shambles and my marriage was in ruins. Pastor Jimmy Jack once again intervened. This time he gave me an ultimatum: I must either go to Pure Life Ministries (PLM), a program for sexual addiction in Kentucky, or be excommunicated from the church.

I was furious with him and even angry at Rose. All I could envision was some weird, hillbilly scene straight out of the movie *Deliverance*. Everything in me was screaming "No!" yet I also knew I was out of options. I reluctantly boarded the bus for Kentucky amidst a blinding snowstorm. In spite of the fact that I arrived at PLM full of anger, pride and confusion, deep inside I also knew that I needed to find God in the worst way. Rose, too, sensed she needed a fresh breakthrough with the Lord. She knew that our marriage was an idol and that she needed to give preeminence to the Lord in her heart. Moreover, she had to face the very real possibility that I would fail again. It was obvious to both of us that we had to put our marriage into His hands.

We needed more than a marriage improvement book. We needed a cleansing of our hearts and a deep spiritual work if we were to have a lasting marriage.

God used my sexual sin as the means to drive us to our knees. In time, He would show us how our circumstances could be used to bring blessings into our lives, but first we needed to learn to love and obey Him. We both had a long way to go, but over time the Lord dramatically changed our lives. We also came to realize that we weren't the only Christian couple facing overwhelming marital problems.

REBUILDING A DEVASTATED MARRIAGE

Internet pornography and sexual sin has flourished in the Church in recent years, destroying innumerable marriages in the process. In an online poll of 10,000 Christians conducted by Focus on the Family several years ago, 47% stated that pornography had been a problem in their home. No doubt this onslaught of sexual sin has played a part in the fact that the divorce rate within Christian homes is hovering around 50 percent—about the same as the rest of our nation. Commenting on this phenomenon, Barna Project director Meg Flammang said: "We would love to be able to report that Christians are living very distinct lives and impacting the community, but in the area of divorce rates they continue to be the same."[1] Christians divorcing at the same rate as unbelievers? Is it possible that we can do no better than the unbelieving world in dealing with our problems?

My own marriage could have easily become one of those statistics. Rose had every reason to divorce me, and she most certainly would have if God had not intervened and performed a miracle. That was over 15 years ago. Since then, I have been privileged to witness countless marriages lifted from the ash heap and transformed into beautiful representations of God's love and forgiveness. That's what can happen when both husband and wife live in repentance and appropriate God's tremendous promises for their lives.

However, I need to make it clear at the outset that the goal of this book is not to sort out the roles of the husband and wife; provide tips for raising godly children; or to encourage more fulfilling romance and sexual intimacy—though we will touch on some of these topics. *The intent here is to demonstrate that only a deep relationship with Jesus Christ can produce a fulfilling marriage.* When both spouses are living in a vibrant and intimate relationship with Him, everything else will fall into place.

Ultimately, marriage is a matter of the heart. If a marriage is to be preserved, then hearts must change. This is where God always does His work in a person's life. And it's amazing how all of the other problems besetting the marriage are somehow resolved as God deals separately with each spouse's heart.

BUILDING BLOCKS OF RESTORATION

In subsequent chapters, you will find that the theme of this book is drawn from Jesus' great Sermon on the Mount. The Beatitudes found in Matthew 5 are meant to become a spiritual foundation in each heart. God can use those building blocks to raise a marriage out of the ashes of sexual sin and into His glory. If the Holy Spirit is allowed to have His way, He will construct a marriage truly reflecting Christ's beauty on earth.

The truth is that the Beatitudes reveal seven states or qualities of the spiritual life that God desires for His people. They also represent seven aspects of His character. It could be compared to the spectrum of colors generated by passing a beam of light through a prism. The light is broken down into seven distinct colors: red, orange, yellow, green, blue, indigo and violet. Just as we can observe that there are seven different colors in the same beam of light, so the Beatitudes enable us to behold and appreciate each of the aspects of God's character individually. He desires His children to reflect these divine qualities in their own lives. This is the greatest reflection of His glory possible.

In his book, *At the Altar of Sexual Idolatry,* Steve Gallagher wrote, "The Beatitudes contain all that is involved in the process of transformation. Those seven verses, Matthew 5:3-9, describe how a person is prepared for repentance, how it unfolds, and the life that accompanies it."[2] In the same way that those seven blessings provide a road to spiritual recovery for a life ruined by sin, so too they provide a blueprint for the restoration of a marriage devastated by sin. Let's take a cursory look at how this process unfolds.

Before this rebuilding process can begin, there must first be a solid foundation. Thus this building project must begin with *poverty of spirit.* God must bring both spouses to an end of their own resources, abilities and strengths in order to accomplish His work in their lives. It is as they stand empty-handed at the foot of the Cross, that He is able to begin the work of rebuilding their lives and marriage.

The first place the Lord begins this marvelous restorative work is teaching each spouse how to focus on his or her own failures, rather than on those of their mate. This awareness of one's sinfulness brings about a sense of godly sorrow: *blessed are those who mourn.* As each spouse acknowledges and repents over their own sin, they become compassionate toward their mate's struggles. This new camaraderie further strengthens the foundation within the marital relationship.

Sinful behavior, and the marital problems that result from it, are ultimately rooted in a lack of submission to God's authority. But the repentance that comes about through godly sorrow humbles the person into a state of *meekness*: a subjection of one's will to the will of Another. As both spouses begin to obey and to actually live God's Word, a new atmosphere fills their home. Mutual support and camaraderie replace the selfishness, defensiveness and finger-pointing.

Inevitably, meekness begets *a hunger for righteousness.* As the couple grows in their desire to please God, Christ is able to reign in the center of the marriage. This new mindset will cause the couple to "seek first the kingdom of God and His righteousness." Couples will need to examine their priorities in life, including how they invest their time and resources. God can only bless a marriage that is in line with His desires. Ultimately, a marriage can only glorify God when both spouses hunger and thirst to be like Jesus.

It is the *merciful* who are promised mercy from God. Most marital problems arise from a selfish preoccupation with one's own rights and desires. However, the process of repentance found in the Beatitudes brings people into the love of God, and this is especially true in the marriage setting. Consequently, rather than each spouse settling into a selfish preoccupation with their own rights and desires, they both learn to consider the needs of the other. "It is more blessed to give than to receive," said Jesus. (Acts 20:34) One of those blessings is that the more each mate shows mercy to the other, the more they are sure to receive in return.

By this point in the process, another fruit of repentance, purity of heart, will emerge. Not only will the *pure in heart* see God, as the beatitude promises, but they will also enjoy freedom from controlling sin. The effects of habitual sin on the marriage are deep and pervasive. As both spouses proceed through the process of repentance, however, sinful attitudes are exposed in the Light. Issues that are buried deep within the heart come to the surface and are dealt with. Little by little their hearts will become purified and they will gain a greater sight of God. What is happening in their individual hearts will also be expressed in the marriage.

Finally, as a couple allows the first six spiritual truths to be worked into them, the last beatitude simply arises as the culmination of all the others in God's transforming process. The closer a person comes to Christ, the more he or she will become what Jesus called a *peacemaker*. Where once strife and disunity permeated the marriage, the couple is now able to reconcile differences and enjoy godly communication with each other. Harmony in the marital relationship is the crowning fruit of a life of repentance.

FOLLOWING THE MAP

The previous section offers a roadmap for the restoration of an ailing marriage. Having a clear-cut path to marital unity should be a great source of encouragement to the sincere husband and wife. However, that map to success is only valuable to the degree that it is actually followed.

Sometimes when we come to God for help, His answers are not what we want to hear. There were times the Pharisees were so frustrated with Jesus' answers that they were ready to kill Him. It takes humility to hear and receive a "hard word." Most couples who have come to Rose and me for counseling through the years have come expressly looking for solutions to their marital problems. Many times, however, what we tell them doesn't sit well with them. Some couples are interested only in a temporal fix for their marriage while God is interested in building His kingdom.

In order to overcome the issues and obstacles that lie ahead, you have to commit yourself to doing things God's way. Rose and I have been counseling for nearly 15 years and we are still amazed at the level of resistance we face from Christians who claim to believe the Word of God. In spite of the fact that our counseling is all based in Scripture, it is amazing how often people respond with statements like, "God wouldn't expect me to do that," or "That's not what Dr. So-and-So wrote in his book." Still others protest, "You don't understand what I have been through." It grieves me to hear these kinds of responses, because I know these people are only evading and prolonging what God needs to do for them.

Sometimes professing Christians look at the words of Jesus and conclude that they are either too hard to follow, or too simple to work. Nevertheless, they are the words of the One who spoke the universe into existence. He is the One who sustains all things by His Word; the One who is the wisdom of God; the One who is the way, the truth and the life; and the One who will bring all things into judgment. What could be more important than conforming our lives and marriages to His Word? Whose opinion can we regard above His?

To put it bluntly, marriages fail because people are unwilling to conform their lives to God's Word. I can tell you that if Rose was determined to take the easy route, we would have ended up in divorce court. There was even a time when I thought divorce was the preferable route. Restoring a marriage is difficult, and the work of restoration nearly always goes against the grain of our natural tendencies. Winning this battle requires people to consistently do things that are uncomfortable.

Yet, if Rose and I had not followed the principles outlined in this book, we would not be where we are today. When we were simply trying to obey the Lord, we had no idea that He would one day use us to help others. We only knew that we needed to be conformed into the likeness of Jesus.

The marriages that we have seen make it through this process are the ones where the couples have embraced the Cross. Please, beloved reader, keep an open mind and a willing heart from the outset; God is calling you to something better than what you can imagine.

Rose and I are continually amazed at the goodness and mercy of God. He has blessed our lives and marriage more than we ever could have imagined. He is a "more than" God: *more than* able, *more than* willing and *more than* sufficient. He always goes beyond our expectations and there are no limits to His offer of mercy. He is "able to do exceedingly abundantly above all that we ask or think, according to the power that works in us..." (Ephesians 3:20)

It is our testimony that, if you will follow the principles this book provides, the Lord will do for you what He has done for us!

"Look at Him; and the more we look
at Him, the more hopeless shall we feel
by ourselves, and in and of ourselves, and
the more shall we become 'poor in spirit.'
Look at Him, keep looking at Him.
Look at the saints, look at the men
who have been most filled with the Spirit
and used. But above all, look again at Him,
and then you will have nothing to do to yourself.
It will be done. You cannot truly look at Him
without feeling your absolute poverty, and
emptiness. Then you say to Him,
'Nothing in my hand I bring,
simply to Thy cross I cling.'"[1]
~ D. Martyn Lloyd-Jones

Chapter Two

LAYING THE FOUNDATION

"Blessed are the poor in spirit, for theirs is the kingdom of heaven." (Matthew 5:3)

A few years ago, Rose and I worked with a couple who had been married for many years. About ten years before we got involved, Keith had committed adultery with another woman. Since that time, even though he had repented of his adultery, they had grown further and further apart. At the point of our involvement, things were at a crisis point and the house was about to fall.

Whenever we tried to focus on the problem, however, an argument would ensue. Each one would explain all that he or she was doing right and would complain about the other's many failures. Sarah, Keith's wife, was bitter with him, feeling as though he didn't love her the way he should. She constantly voiced her grievances to him; in fact, she would openly complain about Keith to other people right in front of him! He was equally resentful over what he saw as Sarah's lack of support for him. He was convinced that he could never make her happy no matter how hard he tried. In his frustration, Keith once again began looking outside of his marriage for the emotional support of another woman.

It was upsetting to watch these two destroy a 40-year marriage and to witness the subsequent pain it caused their children and grandchildren. Even worse, it was truly heart-wrenching to watch as they drove a wedge between themselves and God.

The saddest part of this story was that it didn't have to end this way. It was obvious that if they had been willing to humble themselves, and admit their failures, God could have restored their marriage. Had they each purposed to show unselfishness toward the other, their marriage could have greatly improved. This marriage was not destroyed so much by outward sin as much as by immense pride on both their parts. They both felt that they were right and that it was the other one who was at fault.

In the end, their attitudes could be characterized by a word which carries frightful implications in the spiritual realm: *unwilling*. They were unwilling to humble themselves, unwilling to show Christian charity to each other; in short, they were unwilling to obey God. This is the kind of self-centered living that will make divorce the only option for a struggling marriage.

Wholeness through Brokenness, Wealth through Poverty

What if this couple would have sat down one day and decided that they were going to exert their utmost determination to restore their marriage? Would things have ended differently? It might surprise you to find out that they actually did this very thing. During one of our counseling sessions they both vowed to do whatever it would take to rebuild their shattered relationship. Unfortunately, it wasn't enough. The reason their efforts failed was because they made a fundamental mistake: they tried to do it in their own strength.

Rebuilding a marriage that has been devastated by sexual sin is comparable to climbing a Himalayan mountain without the proper equipment. None of us has the ability to accomplish such an undertaking. Without snowshoes, ice-picks, oxygen tanks and all of the other necessary supplies one needs, it will prove to be a doomed expedition. To make a successful climb, the mountaineer has to have those items which are vital to achieving his goal.

When it comes to rebuilding a shattered marriage, the first step a couple must take is to acknowledge that they do not have the wherewithal within themselves to accomplish it. If their only hope for success is found within themselves, their best efforts are doomed to failure. Ultimately they will end up pointing out the other's failures, just like Keith and Sarah did.

And isn't this true of the Christian life? Doesn't real Christianity begin when a person realizes that he cannot save himself by his own efforts? This was the very point Jesus made by opening the Sermon on the Mount with the first beatitude: "Blessed are the poor in spirit, for theirs is the kingdom of heaven." (Matthew 5:3)

Poverty of spirit was simply Jesus' way of saying that a person has come to an end of himself. He comes to see his desperate need for salvation but, much to his horror, when he looks within to find an answer to his terrifying dilemma, he discovers that he doesn't have the spiritual wherewithal to save himself. He prostrates himself in the dust and cries out for mercy to God. Only the blood of Jesus Christ can provide the necessary atonement for his sins. It is this same sense of destitution that causes a couple to look to God alone to salvage the marriage their sin has destroyed.

Rose and I knew that there was nothing to be gained in trying to rebuild our shattered marriage on the old foundation. We recognized that we needed a new foundation: one that was built upon the solid bedrock of Christ. If a couple isn't willing to start here, they will find that their attempt to rebuild their marriage will be no more successful than a carpenter building a house on a sand foundation. It simply will not stand.

We quickly found out that we simply didn't have the desire

or ability to do it on our own. We fully understood our desperate need for Him. This kind of desperation is always found in those who understand their inability. It also describes what it means to be "poor in spirit."

Poverty of spirit is the same lowly attitude one sees in a child. It is the state of continual dependence in which one knows he has nothing, can do nothing, and wants nothing but Jesus. This attitude is what Jesus was referring to when He said, "Assuredly, I say to you, unless you are converted and become as little children, you will by no means enter the kingdom of heaven." (Matthew 18:2-3)

Albert Barnes rightly said: "To be poor in spirit is to have a humble opinion of ourselves; to be sensible that we are sinners, and have no righteousness of our own; to be willing to be saved only by the rich grace and mercy of God; to be willing to be where God places us, to bear what he lays on us, to go where he bids us;…to be willing to be in his hands, and to feel that we deserve no favor from him. It is the complete absence of pride, and vanity, and ambition."[2]

One cannot produce poverty of spirit in oneself; it is simply a vivid awareness of one's utter helplessness. It is the awakening of the heart to the wonder of just Jesus Christ Himself. There is an old hymn that expresses how a sinner finds everything he or she needs in Him:

> Oh to be nothing, nothing; only to lie at His feet,
> A broken and emptied vessel; for the Master's use made meet.
> Emptied that He might fill me; as forth to His service I go,
> Broken, that so unhindered; His life through me might show.
>
> Oh to be nothing, nothing; only as led by His hand,
> A messenger at His gateway; only waiting for His command.
> Only an instrument ready; His praises to sound at His will,
> Willing should He not require me; in silence to wait on Him still.

Oh to be nothing, nothing; painful the humbling may be,
Yet low in the dust I'd lay me; that the world might my Savior see.
Rather be nothing, nothing; to Him let our voices be raised,
He is the fountain of blessing; He only is meet to be praised.[3]

You won't find this tune on the Top Ten list of Christian radio hits! Nevertheless, it perfectly describes the cry of the lowly in heart. It also describes the attitude of two people who are building their marriage on the Rock. You see, a truly godly marriage is made up of two sinners, who in their utter helplessness come to God and find all their help in Him. Just like a child totally trusts mommy and daddy for everything he needs, the one who is poor in spirit looks to God for the help he needs.

SIMPLY TO THE CROSS WE CLING

As I said before, it didn't take Rose and me long to realize that we needed help outside of ourselves to be able to fulfill our marriage vows to one another. "For better or worse," we had said; but when both partners become accustomed to experiencing the "worse" rather than the "better," only the grace of God can get them through. We were in the "worse" part of the marriage vow; the terrible bump in the marriage road that sends many couples careening into divorce court.

Even though I had repented of my sexual sin, we still had a lot of issues we were facing. We had to learn the secret of becoming beggars before God. We had to become like the blind man outside of Jericho pleading, "Son of David, have mercy on me!" We had to become like the woman with the issue of blood needing to touch the Savior's cloak. We had to become like Lazarus in the tomb, awaiting the call from the Prince of Life.

Everything we held dear had to be relinquished. This included our own idea of what our marriage should be; it

included letting go of what we believed about ourselves; and
it meant forsaking everything we had put our trust in outside
of God. Our *modus operandi* took a 180 degree turn. Then, in
the midst of such complete internal upheaval, God insisted on
bringing us to Pure Life Ministries to work as interns!

Leaving our home in New York City, our family, our
friends—everything familiar—to come to a rural ridge in
Kentucky was a huge challenge. Had we maintained our lives
in New York—where we could stay in control and have things
just the way we wanted them—we would have surely failed. But
coming to Pure Life Ministries to work was part of God's plan
to bring us to the end of our own resources. By depriving us
of everything else, He brought us to an even deeper level of
brokenness.

Beloved, God knows exactly what it will take to bring
us to an end of ourselves—where we will turn to Him for
everything we need. He isn't waiting for us to count up our
resources and conclude that we have enough to make it; He's
fully anticipating that we will conclude that we have absolutely
nothing to contribute. Poverty of spirit isn't being poor in the
sense of having just enough to get by; poverty of spirit means
empty, bankrupt, utterly destitute.

After completing my time in the Pure Life Ministries
residential program, it was tempting to conclude that Rose and
I had gotten everything we needed. We were anxious to get on
with "real" life, and to have a "real" marriage. But by following
God's call to move to Kentucky He was able to keep us in that
place of neediness for Him.

That doesn't mean that we didn't have difficulties and
setbacks. Resuming our on-again, off-again marriage would
have been difficult under any circumstances. Just dealing with
the marital issues was plenty but, on top of all that, we were
working at a ministry where the staff all lived together on the

same property. It was most definitely like being in the proverbial fish bowl. Our lives were open to inspection by everyone around us. Then, as if all that were not enough, there was an atmosphere of high expectations. We were expected to maintain a high level of spiritual consecration. To be sure, God was dealing with us in many areas and at all levels of our spiritual lives.

He often used ordinary things to show us how much we desperately needed Him. One example of this was the occasion when Rose and I were directed to drive down to Tennessee to get a pickup truck someone had donated to the ministry. No big deal, right? Well, when we got there, it wasn't just any ordinary old pickup. The truck was previously owned by a race car mechanic. He had installed a bored out, "worked-to-the-bone" Corvette engine in it, complete with headers and side pipes. It was fire engine red, had chrome mag wheels, and an array of gauges on the dashboard resembling the cockpit of a race car. In my unconquered condition, I couldn't wait to get behind the wheel.

As I climbed aboard the truck, Rose slipped into our car behind me. I immediately gunned it, leaving "a little rubber" as I sped down the street to the stop sign. My wife quickly got alongside and yelled out the window "What are you doing?"

Who, me? What did I do? (I should probably confess right here that about a week prior to this I was kind of congratulating myself on how God had really helped me with my anger.) As soon as the words came out of my wife's mouth, my blood began to boil and I immediately punched the gas and sped off down the road again, literally leaving her in a small cloud of dust. When I stopped at the next intersection, she *again* pulled up alongside of me and expressed her disappointment about the way I was acting. That was it! I proceeded to get out of the truck and tell her off, using some easily recalled curse words that I hadn't used for a long time. Then, when she burst into tears,

I really let her have it! It was the old Jeff in rare form. I was so mad I was shaking and ready to leave her behind.

After a little while, God somehow calmed me down. I repented to Rose and we started to make our way back to Kentucky. It was one of the longest drives I have ever taken. All I could see was how I had blown it, leaving me to wonder whether God had accomplished anything inside me. I felt like I would never be able to be the husband the Lord wanted me to be. Needless to say, it was very humbling, but in the end it brought me back to where I needed to be: right at His feet.

I want to say this as humbly as I can, but there is an important truth that begs sharing. If Keith and Sarah had ended their conflicts with this type of repentance and neediness before God, their story would have ended much differently. It is our poverty of spirit that invites the riches of God's mercy and grace into these difficult situations. The pickup truck incident I shared is just one of many times Rose and I needed God to intervene. Many times we have needed Him to pour out His mercy and rescue us from ourselves. But I also know that the Bible teaches that God is drawn to the lowly—the one who is willing to repent.

Our need for God's intervention didn't end after the intern program at Pure Life Ministries either. I can't tell you how many times He has had to bring me back to the foot of the Cross over the years. You see, just because we had completed a program didn't mean that everything was going to be "peaches and cream" now. A lot of couples who come to us for help think that when the counseling program is over everything is going to be wonderful. As you can see, however, I still had a lot of rough edges—inside and out. To this day there are still times when I look in the mirror and see the old wretch staring back at me.

Sometimes, a couple's expectations can be a little high—or even a lot high. Wives envision a godly husband who is literally

Jesus walking around the house. He will never have a bad thought again or be tempted to look at another woman. He will place her on a pedestal in his heart to worship and adore. He will be sweet, kind, and patient with her at all times. He will be happy to sit and talk with her for hours, intently listening to everything she has to say. He will be affectionate and loving to her, never allowing her to feel neglected or unimportant. He will bring heaven down to earth in their home. Best of all, she will be able to boast to everybody what a godly husband she has.

Likewise, the husband envisions a godly wife who submits to him without any resistance. She will always praise him, compliment him and build him up. She will be quiet and gentle in spirit. She will never question him about anything, because she trusts in his wisdom. She will always be in the mood to make love, because her greatest desire is to please her husband.

Beloved, this isn't Fantasyland! It's real life! The reality is that a godly husband and wife are two redeemed sinners who simply see their need for God. And even though they fail at times, possibly many times, they will always be willing to repent and come back to the Cross of Christ. They will continue to allow God to change them, and as time goes by, there will be less of them, and more of Jesus. They will decrease, and He will increase. (John 3:30)

Rose wasn't exempt from God's process either. She was dealing with the very real emotional trauma of leaving all that she knew in New York, including her friends, her church, her family and a job that she had been at for 14 years. She was also in culture shock. I remember the day we arrived from New York. She got out of the car and the ministry's cook—a lady from Alabama with an extreme southern drawl—quickly came over to greet her. She talked to her for quite some time while Rose just smiled and nodded her head. Then we proceeded into our new living quarters. When we walked into the room, Rose immediately burst into tears and said, "Does everybody talk like that down here? I didn't understand a word she said!" She was truly a fish out of water.

Not surprisingly, Rose was overwhelmed at times with the various aspects of both coming to work for the ministry as well as coming back together with her husband, the same man who had dragged her through the mud for years. I remember one morning walking into the house after a prayer walk and finding her sitting in her chair crying as she prayed through Psalm 119. I asked her what was wrong and all she could manage to choke out, with the deepest of reality in her words, was, "I'm just dust." God had been using her situation, and the teachings she had been going through, to show her that she was just a pile of dust before Him. It is a powerful revelation that few experience, but it is the very attitude that kept Rose committed to a marriage many would have long since given up on.

KNOWING WHERE TO TURN

As believers, we are called to emulate the life of Jesus Christ. We are all called to walk as He walked and to love others as He loved us. That can seem like a tall order, yet God commands it; something He wouldn't do if it were not possible.

Yet, how many times I have heard counselees say, "I can't do this!" Well, it's true! That's my point: You can't do it! But God can, if we will but learn how to acknowledge what we are...Helpless!!! This is one of the foundational laws of Christianity. "God resists the proud, but gives grace to the humble." (I Peter 5:5) Or, stated another way: "Whoever exalts himself will be humbled, and he who humbles himself will be exalted." (Matthew 23:12)

It is true, the husband cannot, in his own power, bear his wife through her painful memories and vacillating fits of anger, bitterness and fear. He simply does not have it in himself to be the priest and the husband that God has called him to be. Loving one's wife as Christ loved the church cannot be done in the flesh.

Likewise, the wife cannot forgive her husband, learn to make herself vulnerable again or be a godly, loving wife in her own strength. Both partners can memorize Scriptural references on marriage and study the roles of each spouse, but if they don't actually live out these verses, then all they have is head knowledge. Without accessing the power of God through poverty of spirit, they are left with no possible way to live out the tenets of Scripture toward their spouse.

Are you beginning to grasp how blessed it is to be poor in spirit? Seeing your poverty is the prerequisite to accessing God's riches—and He is rich in grace and mercy! (Ephesians 1:7, 2:4) And these are the very things your marriage desperately needs.

There are many things that will keep a couple defeated and unable to overcome the difficulties and challenges they are facing in the process of restoration. Undoubtedly, one of the most common is self-righteousness. Wives especially are vulnerable to this form of pride. It is very easy to remain fixated on obvious forms of wickedness, such as sexual sin. But God sees within the heart, where selfish attitudes lurk, such as envy, hatred and pride. A believer who holds an exaggerated evaluation of his or her spiritual progress will not be able to discern their own areas of need. Self-righteousness is a pernicious attitude that keeps people from seeing their need to live in daily repentance before God.

The belief in oneself, one's own achievements and the accuracy of one's own judgments is the very thing that will keep a believer away from Jesus. A person cannot trust both Jesus and himself. His only hope is for God to bring him down to a place of brokenness and poverty, the place where he was at the beginning of his Christian walk.

No one can be the husband or wife God wants them to be if they hold onto something that defeats them. That very thing which defeats many is the reign of Self in the heart. I challenge you to say, "*God, yank it out of me. You be the Ruler of my heart. Help me to learn to live in lowly dependence upon You.*" These are the words you'll need to pray if you expect to see God's power at work in your heart, your life and your marriage.

Secondly, you will need to earnestly pray over the words of Jesus until you can do all of them toward your spouse. Most husbands I have dealt with in counseling become intimidated when they see what the Bible says about their duties to their wives. They feel like they will never be able to measure up. The wives often feel the same way about their role. However, when they learn the secret of His strength being perfected in weakness, hope floods their souls. Then they can look up at His face and say, "*Jesus I want to stay right here, until You help me to do what You have commanded me. I believe You can make me the husband or the wife You intend me to be.*"

If you will pray over the words of Christ, you will find out quickly just how badly you need God's provision to enable you to live those words. The truth is that you need to be filled with the Holy Spirit if you have any hope of living the words of Jesus. However, you cannot be filled with the Holy Spirit until you are emptied of Self.

Lastly, you need to pray for a fresh sight of Calvary. As the familiar hymn says: "At the Cross, at the Cross where I *first* saw the light" (emphasis added). It is always there at the cross where we first saw the light that we will continue to see the light. When we lose sight of Calvary and what Jesus did there, we lose the sight of Him who is all our hope and righteousness. May we never boast, except in the Cross of Jesus Christ.

Before a marriage can be rebuilt, both parties must start at the same place. Are you willing to be an impoverished beggar before God? When both partners are living at the foot of the cross, there won't be any finger pointing. The more you look at the Cross, the more you will see Jesus and be content to have just Him. "The Cross is proof that there is no length to which the love of God will refuse to go, in order to win men's hearts. If the Cross will not waken love and wonder in men's hearts, nothing will."[4] With a fresh sight of Calvary, you will want to thank Jesus for His precious blood, and you will be in your first love where everything you do is for Him. Your expectations upon your spouse will diminish because Jesus will be preeminent in your heart.

Rose and I had to start here at the Cross and we will end here at this same place. This is not a one time event. A godly marriage starts at the foot of the Cross and continues right on living there in all God's mercy and grace. As one author has put it, "If one feels anything in the presence of God save an utter poverty of spirit, it ultimately means that you have never faced Him. That is the meaning of this Beatitude."[5] Poverty of spirit is the foundation that God must have to bring any marriage to the place He intends it to be. You need Him!

DANNY AND PAULA

*P*aula grew up in a godly Christian home. Her parents led her and her sister in family devotions and had them in church three times a week. They even kept a tight rein on television viewing in the home. The girls flourished in this environment, eventually becoming leaders in their youth group.

Paula was reserved by nature, which caused her to be cautious about opening up to others. "I was afraid that if someone really knew my struggles that I might be rejected," she recalls. "Instead, I sought acceptance by trying to do good, look good and be good." The unfortunate side effect of this outlook was a growing attitude of self-righteousness. "When it came to my relationship with Christ, I thought that since I was 'good,' I *deserved* my salvation. The Cross was reserved for 'sinners.'"

One Sunday morning a new guy showed up in Paula's college-age Sunday school class. Danny was funny, handsome and charismatic. Eventually the two became inseparable. For the first time in her life Paula felt like she could really open up her heart to another person. Danny's kindness and empathy overcame her natural caution. He, too, shared his heart with her. One of the things that came out of these meaningful conversations was that he had had a problem with pornography and sexual sin in the past. "Things are different now," he reassured her.

"I believed him because I wanted to believe him," Paula now says, looking back. Danny was fun and exciting. Her growing admiration for him led her to make foolish and sinful decisions, which eventually included premarital sex. "It is amazing how easily I excused my behavior away, even though I knew in my heart that it was wrong."

Nevertheless, the young couple was soon married. But Paula quickly discovered that this would be no fairytale marriage. "It was soon obvious that Danny had never left the world of sexual sin," she says. It began with finding pornography on his computer. Later, she discovered text-messaging conversations he was having with other women on the Internet. The final blow came when Paula found out he had committed adultery with a girl from work.

The sense of betrayal Paula felt ran very deep. She had finally made herself vulnerable to another person and he had broken her heart. Gradually, a root of bitterness began to develop within her heart, not only toward Danny, but also toward the Lord for "letting this happen."

For thirteen years the couple had to deal with the consequences of Danny's obsession with sex. Every fresh revelation of his sinful activity would throw the two into another round of turmoil. Each time he would tearfully repent and make sincere-sounding promises to change. But the godly home Paula had envisioned was turning into "a hell on earth."

One day, something snapped inside her. She had had enough. It would be better for her and the three children if Danny would leave. Paula closed her heart to him. She was finished with this marriage.

Danny found himself having to move in with his parents. His father was a minister and a personal friend of Steve Gallagher, the founder of Pure Life Ministries (PLM). When the truth came out about Danny's sin, his father was quick to point him to (PLM).

Danny showed up in Kentucky broken over the loss of his wife and kids but very much out of touch with true Christianity. Danny's smooth and charismatic personality had made it possible for him to blend with true believers and to play the part of a "Christian," but the truth was that he had never really known the Lord for himself. At PLM, he was forced to acknowledge his sin—not just his immoral behavior but his lost and sinful condition as a member of the fallen human race. It felt as though the bottom dropped out from beneath him. He cried out to God for forgiveness and repented of his sins. In short, he was born again! He began seeking the Lord in a real and meaningful way. He was excited to be a Christian!

To his great regret, Paula was unwilling to participate in the telephone counseling program that PLM offered wives. And so it came as no surprise when, three months into the program, he received divorce papers from her. This was Danny's first big challenge as a believer. How would he react to this? Would he give up and throw himself back into pursuing sexual experiences? No, he continued to press into the Lord. By the time he graduated the Live-In program, he was truly a changed man.

In the meantime, Paula was at home trying to make ends meet, holding down a job, raising the kids… and languishing in a "victim's mentality."

Before she knew it, Danny was back in town. It quickly became obvious to her that he was a new person. He treated her and the kids with a kindness and compassion she hadn't seen since they were dating. Actually, Paula could sense a level of sincerity that was different from what she had experienced from him during their courtship. She was happy for him but had no intention or desire to reconcile.

For his part, Danny was just determined to maintain his walk with God and show his family true, godly love. In spite of the fact that he remained a consistent Christian and loving father, there was no change in Paula's attitude toward him.

The truth was that Paula was in trouble spiritually. By constantly nurturing her grievances against Danny and even the Lord, she was able to justify doing things she knew were wrong. "I was heading down a dark road of selfishness and self-entitlement that led to inappropriate relationships and the pursuit of material goods," she recalls. "I tried to excuse my behavior away, saying that, after all that I had been through, I deserved to have some fun. But I knew I was on a dark path and was only becoming more miserable." Paula was in a spiritual freefall.

Her spiritual decline did not go unnoticed by Danny. He knew she was in trouble, but he was also painfully aware of the fact that he was not in any position to talk to her about it. Of course, since the day he received his divorce papers he had been fervently praying for reconciliation, but he gradually became more concerned about her spiritual well-being than any hopes of remarriage. Danny quietly prayed and put Paula in God's hands.

In the meantime, by sheer "coincidence," Steve and Kathy Gallagher had been booked to speak in Paula's church. It was October, 2007, nearly three years after he arrived home from PLM that Paula told Danny they were coming. "I'm going to a conference this weekend at the church," she blandly told him. "It's being put on by that place in Kentucky where you went. What was it called, 'Pure Life' or something?"

He couldn't believe it! "I was on my way home from work when she told me this and I nearly drove off the road at the news!" Danny remembers. "I began praying my heart out."

"Actually, I went to the seminar out of a selfish curiosity," Paula admits. "I listened to Kathy Gallagher speak that morning, but I had become so hardhearted and prideful that I didn't pay much attention."

For some reason, however, Paula did feel compelled to remain after the seminar was over. There was a line of ladies who wanted to talk to Kathy, and Paula inexplicably stood with them, ostensibly waiting to thank her for "a job well done." Suddenly, it was her turn. The two sat down next to each other and Paula's mind went blank. She somehow was able to briefly share about Danny's time at Pure Life and their divorce. "I don't know why I'm here," she kept saying to Kathy. Something powerful was churning inside her.

"I know why you're here, Paula," Kathy calmly told her. "God is dealing with you about unforgiveness. He has called you here today for a purpose. He is greater than your problems. Don't underestimate what He can do for you."

Paula thanked her and hurried out the door. "I couldn't get to my van soon enough, where I broke down in tears and repented to God for my sin. I was not worthy of *anything*. He died for *all* of our sins. I was not without sin. In fact, I was full of sin, bitterness, pride and falsehood. I had spent my entire life pushing people away to protect myself. Now I realized I needed to truly let Christ into my heart and my life, surrender to Him and let Him have complete control. Only then could I experience true peace and happiness."

As she sat there sobbing uncontrollably, she suddenly knew inside that the Lord was going to restore their marriage. During the past two years, Danny's mother had invited Paula to join the family for Thanksgiving dinner. Each year she had politely declined. Danny's mother was going to call her again this year, but he stopped her. "It won't do any good, Mom."

This time it was Paula who made the phone call. She asked Danny's mother if she and the kids were still welcome. "Of course," was the gracious reply. That day, new feelings for Danny emerged in Paula's heart that she had assumed would never come back. The two began dating again. Instead of being physical with each other, they would spend hours talking about the things of God. The relationship that was built during that time was completely different from the original one.

Paula was so determined to make sure everything was done right this time that she enrolled in the PLM counseling program for wives. Rose worked with her over the next three months, helping her to see how to turn to the Lord in her own need. Eventually, the two were remarried. Then they did something completely unexpected. "We moved to Kentucky—the place where we found new life!" God truly became the center of their marriage.

"It is by His grace alone that I am here today to say how GREAT is our God and how blessed I am to have a healthy relationship with Him, as well as with my husband. *Thank you, Jesus!*" she exclaims.

"Words cannot express the difference in our relationship," Danny adds. "The Lord has done a work in our hearts that neither of us could have imagined! His Word is true; He really does make all things New!!!"

*"To bear the cross simply, without letting your
self-love add all sorts of dilemmas to it, will make
your life easier. When you accept the Cross and simply
allow it to do the work God intended, you will be happy
because you will see what good fruit is produced in you.
When you love God, it will not matter to you what
you must suffer on His behalf. The Cross will
make you over in the image of your Beloved."*[1]

~ François Fénelon

Chapter Three

EMBRACING CHRIST'S SUFFERING

"Blessed are those who mourn, for they shall be comforted."
(Matthew 5:4)

*V*alerie's husband had been unrepentant over his sexual sin for years. His sin had brought about a great deal of turmoil in their marriage, eventually causing her to separate from Phil. They eventually entered the Overcomers At-Home program offered by Pure Life Ministries. By this point, Valerie had become a bitter woman with a nasty temper. She had become so miserable that she couldn't even force a smile with people.

Undoubtedly many people would feel that her husband's behavior justified Valerie's attitude. Nevertheless, Rose worked with her week after week, helping her to see how unlike Christ she was being in her response to Phil's sin. Gradually, this dear woman began to break. She started to see how she had allowed her husband's sin to harden her heart. Her unmerciful attitude was driving a wedge between herself and God. Valerie had allowed his sin to steal her joy and her sense of God's presence. Eventually she completely repented of her un-Christlike attitudes. Even though she still occasionally lapses back into old ruts of thinking, she has learned to repent and to turn to God.

I recently saw her at Pure Life Ministries' annual conference and she was beaming with the joy of the Lord. Even though her husband has still not repented of his ongoing sin, she has learned to respond to the suffering with a godly attitude. The joy that is displayed in her life is a powerful testimony to what the Holy Spirit can do inside someone who is willing to repent of their own sins.

MOURNING THE ONE IN THE MIRROR

There are different aspects to the spirit of mourning and suffering, and we will examine several in this chapter. However, the primary aspect is *mourning over one's own sin.* Unless a person is willing to allow God to show him or her what is wrong in their own heart, they will never experience God's comfort. Each spouse must face the Cross for themselves in this journey of restoration. That means that they both must live in the reality of their own shortcomings and sins and continually turn to God in repentance. If they lose sight of the Cross, they will lose the ability to bear each other. When a person lives with the reality of the Cross, he becomes very aware of his own wretched condition and, in a sense, blind to the sins committed by others. But he will also understand the precious blood that will take away his sin and reconcile him to God.

The spirit of mourning is a natural progression for those who have experienced poverty of spirit. One beatitude naturally leads to the next. Poverty of spirit leads a person to mourn over their own sinful condition. "Jesus is speaking about life in the kingdom of God," says Sinclair Ferguson, referring to the Beatitudes. "The poverty He describes is in a man's spirit, not his pocket. Similarly, the grief Jesus describes is man's mourning over his own sinfulness; it is regret that he has proved a disappointment to the Lord. Numbed by the discovery of his poverty of spirit, he learns to grieve because of it."[2]

Those who make temporal happiness the great aim of their lives will never enjoy the blessings of God. The only blessings they will receive will be those they can somehow grant to themselves. And isn't this kind of teaching prevalent in the Church today? In spite of the fact that "seeker-friendly" Christians generally avoid the subject of personal sin, the Bible is very clear about the fact that there is a progressive nature of the Holy Spirit's dealings with man that necessitates conviction of sin, grief over sin and repentance of sin. "Draw near to God and He will draw near to you," James wrote. "Cleanse your hands, you sinners; and purify your hearts, you double-minded. Lament and mourn and weep! Let your laughter be turned to mourning and your joy to gloom. Humble yourselves in the sight of the Lord, and He will lift you up." (James 4:8-10)

We see this resistance to acknowledging one's sin in much of our marital counseling. I have counseled with husbands who simply want their wives to get into Pure Life Ministries' Overcomers At-Home program so they will stop venting their anger. They think their wives should just forgive them and move on as if nothing has happened. Men who have truly experienced grief over how their sin has affected God and others do not think this way.

On the other hand, we also deal with wives who feel that all of the problems in the marriage can be attributed to their husbands. They become upset when they receive the materials from our counseling program, wondering why in the world they have to go through a book called *The Walk of Repentance*. They will typically make a statement that goes something like this: "My husband is the one with the problem, not me! I have nothing to repent about! I have been walking with God for years!"

How different has been the attitude of my wife Rose. In the writing of this book, I discovered an excerpt from her journal, written at a time when she could have easily been focusing on the many sins which I had committed against her.

"All day I have been repenting of me, seeing my need to change, and how much pride I have. The Lord is putting

something in me to death and replacing it with a desire
to be nothing. Nothing else matters but to know Jesus
and to have Him in His fullness."

Rose, like Valerie, has tapped into the blessings that Jesus
Christ promises to those who grieve over their sinful condition.
But how can a person be "blessed" when he or she is suffering?
This seems like an impossible contradiction! Yes, that is exactly
what it is. "Blessed are those who mourn," is one of the divine
paradoxes of the Kingdom of God. Martyn Lloyd-Jones
explains it this way:

> If we truly mourn, we shall rejoice, we shall be made
> happy, we shall be comforted. For it is when a man
> sees himself in this unutterable hopelessness that the
> Holy Spirit reveals unto him the Lord Jesus Christ as
> his perfect satisfaction…That is the astounding thing
> about the Christian life. Your great sorrow leads to joy,
> and without the sorrow there is no joy.[3]

WORLDLY SORROW, GODLY SORROW

The apostle Paul had a clear grasp of the role that sorrow
plays in the process of repentance. Consider what he wrote,
"For godly sorrow produces repentance leading to salvation, not
to be regretted; but the sorrow of the world produces death."
(II Corinthians 7:10) In this passage of Scripture, Paul adds
something to this subject that wasn't brought out in the second
beatitude: while some people experience godly sorrow over
their sin, others experience something which he calls "worldly
sorrow."

King Saul, like so many people today, experienced this type
of shallow repentance. When confronted by Samuel the Prophet
about disobeying the Lord, he made excuses and resorted to

blame-shifting. He minimized his sin by pointing out that it was his soldiers who took the things which God said should have been utterly destroyed. When he finally did acknowledge his sin, his confession utterly lacked any sense of sincere remorse. He said, "I have sinned; yet honor me now, please, before the elders of my people and before Israel, and return with me, that I may worship the Lord your God." (I Samuel 15:30) In other words, "Okay; I know I blew it; but can we just move on from this so I won't have to experience any consequences?" This was a shallow, worldly sorrow at best, and it is important to remember that God did not accept Saul's repentance.

I prompt you now, dear reader, to consider your own perspective of the sin in your life. Please don't lose sight of the fact that this disastrous episode began Saul's downward spiral. After Saul's lack of true repentance, he was beset with bouts of mental anguish and demonic torment. His envy of God's anointed successor, David, resulted in fits of rage, attempted murder, and ostracizing his son Jonathan. Saul became obsessed with pursuing David, along the way murdering the priests of Nob and seeking assistance from the witch at En Dor. Finally he died, along with three of his sons, on Mount Gilboa. All of these tragic events were connected to his lack of repentance. There is a price to pay if we only look at others' sins and not our own.

Unfortunately, I see this tepid sorrow in many of the men I encounter in my travels for Pure Life Ministries. Steve Gallagher, the founder of Pure Life Ministries has written: "Worldly sorrow is the grief due to unfavorable circumstances. Sexual sin can quickly bring such circumstances about. Financial debts often pile up; a devastated wife may disappear with the children; or a secret life may be exposed on the job or even in the church. Some may even face criminal charges for their actions. Feeling tremendous remorse over one's actions because of the consequences that have followed is not uncommon."[4] But remorse over consequences is not repentance.

The Bible contrasts worldly sorrow with godly sorrow. Just as we could see worldly sorrow in King Saul's life, we can see a picture of godly sorrow in the life of his successor, King David. When confronted with his sin with Bathsheba, all David could see was how black his heart was. Consider how different is his response from that of Saul:

> For I acknowledge my transgressions, and my sin is always before me. Against You, You only, have I sinned, and done this evil in Your sight—that You may be found just when You speak, and blameless when You judge. Behold, I was brought forth in iniquity, and in sin my mother conceived me. Behold, You desire truth in the inward parts, and in the hidden part You will make me to know wisdom. Purge me with hyssop, and I shall be clean; wash me, and I shall be whiter than snow. Make me hear joy and gladness, that the bones You have broken may rejoice. Hide Your face from my sins, and blot out all my iniquities. Create in me a clean heart, O God, and renew a steadfast spirit within me. Do not cast me away from Your presence, and do not take Your Holy Spirit from me. Restore to me the joy of Your salvation, and uphold me by Your generous Spirit. (Psalm 51:3-12)

This is a true picture of what the apostle Paul later called godly sorrow. David wasn't concerned about losing his position as king, being dishonored before man, or any other consequence that might result from his actions. His only concern was that God would not take His Spirit from him.

True remorse over one's sin always has this same quality about it. It is simply clear then that the man who only wants to get back into the good graces of his wife and is looking to avoid the consequences of his sin, hasn't experienced godly sorrow. If a husband has truly repented he will be willing to embrace the suffering that accompanies repentance, no matter how painful.

Paul went on to give a fuller description of godly sorrow to the Corinthians: "what earnestness this godly grief has produced in you, what eagerness to clear yourselves, what indignation, what alarm, what longing, what zeal, what punishment! At every point you have proved yourselves guiltless in the matter." (II Corinthians 7:11 NRSV) Let's take a few minutes to examine these fruits of godly sorrow a bit more closely.

- *Earnestness:* Could also mean diligence or eagerness; this refers to the initial effect of repentance. It means to end indifference; a decision has been made; a line has been crossed—repentance has been carried over the threshold in one's life.

- *Clearing of yourselves:* The person no longer wants to be known, and is beginning to no longer be known, for his or her former sin. One's life looks differently because of concentrated and sustained effort on the part of the individual; the stigma associated with one's sin is deteriorating.

- *Indignation:* Righteous anger over one's past life and the ramifications his or her sin has caused; residual shame still lingers, perhaps even anger over current struggles associated with former sins; this also extends to righteous anger over sin in general as more and more light is introduced into the repentant person's life.

- *Alarm:* Fear of God, His discipline, His wrath and judgment. This reverence increases as repentance grows; it is the beginning of wisdom, since He is the One most grieved by the sin.

- *Longing*: At the heart level, one's affections are changing, deliberately shifting toward God and away from past sins and sinful longings. Those things that captivated the person no longer do.

- *Zeal*: Growing affection for God and His people so that solid hatred for the world takes root; consuming desire for God has replaced anything that stole this in the past.

- *Punishment*: A willingness to go through the fire of discipline, pain, or judgment, in order that one's sin is justly punished as God allows. When a person has the previous fruits of godly sorrow, this must follow. When someone wants Jesus so much, and He is their goal and affection, then punishment and discipline, though painful, are mere tools in His hand to draw this person to Himself. The individual doesn't mind going through it; indeed, he or she is grateful for it.

Allow me to share one last thought on this issue of godly versus worldly sorrow before we move on. The Bible provides the perfect illustration of Heaven's dividing line between the two in the story found in Luke 18. If you recall, two men went up to the temple to pray; one was a Pharisee and the other a tax collector. The Pharisee approached God, undoubtedly in the same manner he always did. He thanked Him that he wasn't like others, especially in light of this tax collector next to him—a man who was obviously a sinner. The Pharisee congratulated himself on himself, glorying in his distinctions as he saw them. "I fast twice a week; I give tithes of all that I possess. I'm not like the others, unjust, extortioners, adulterers, or even as this publican." It should go without saying that there is nothing wrong with fasting or tithing. The problem is that something was missing from his prayer, which consequently changed his whole position before God. We find that missing ingredient in the prayer of the publican who stood afar off and "would not lift up so much as his eyes unto heaven, but smote upon his breast saying, 'God be merciful to me a sinner!' "I tell you," said the Divine Judge; "this man went down to his house justified." (Luke 18:9-14) The one who had God's attention here was the one who understood what it meant to mourn over his sin. Can you see how the mourning tax collector is utterly unaware of the sin of the other? Indeed, he can scarcely bear to stand before God without addressing every reason why God should not hear him! This man knew how to mourn. And most significantly, he left comforted and forgiven.

ENTERING INTO CHRIST'S SUFFERINGS

Not too long ago, I heard the story of a couple who live nearby who had videotaped the husband raping his two-year-old daughter and then posted the video on the Internet. My heart was grieved and mad at the same time when I heard this story: grieved for that innocent little girl and mad at the people who could do such a thing. For days, I couldn't shake from my mind what I had heard. My anger grew. They had to pay for what they had done! Then something unexpected happened to me. The thought came to me that Jesus had witnessed this entire incident; the pure Lamb of God had to watch this horrible act as it happened. As I considered this, it dawned on me that He has to watch everything that happens on our planet. It was this kind of behavior that was in the Cup He had to drink in the Garden of Gethsemane. The thought of all of this brought me to tears. I wanted to put my arm around Jesus and say to

Him, "Lord, I will endure this with You." Then He asked me something that caught me off guard: "Will you mourn over the husband and wife with Me like you are mourning for the little girl? I died for them too." It was too much for me to take; nevertheless, I knew it was true. I was taken aback by the enormous compassion and mercy of God that is extended to the worst of sinners. It went beyond human logic. As I began to pray for the husband and wife, my anger toward them gave way to God's heart of compassion.

Dear ones, our mourning doesn't stop with ourselves. Wouldn't it be self-centered to think only of our own sins being forgiven without considering those around us who are still perishing? Wouldn't it be selfish not to mourn for them? Believe me, God is mourning for them.

Now bring this thought back to your marriage. How do you view your spouse's sin? Do you see how it will harm him or her, or only how it is affecting you? Jesus can only see how our sin is harming our own souls. Isn't that the attitude He exhibited at Calvary? God's compassion compels us to willingly enter into the suffering of another so that we can bear them to the throne of God. That kind of unselfishness is what makes a good marriage.

Sometimes spouses set limits on one another as to what they will put up with. I have heard wives say, "If he ever falls into sin again, or even looks at another woman again, it's over." Yet she has no concern about allowing her pride, gossip, criticism or resentment continue unchecked in her heart. Some husbands are the same. As long as a man isn't in his sin to the same degree he was formerly, he thinks he is in good standing with God. And even though his heart is still full of lust, he is quick to point out his wife's faults. It is so often the case that a husband or wife can overlook the log in their own eye for the speck in their spouse's eye. If Jesus was that way with any of us, we would be instantly destroyed.

Now, it goes without saying that when dealing with a man in sexual sin there is a point when a line must be drawn in the sand. Rose did that when I was in my sin. But it is another thing when the husband is sincerely trying, yet occasionally still struggles. To expect a man to never again entertain a lustful thought is not realistic. If he is sincerely seeking the Lord, his heart will gradually become purified. Likewise, the husband must have patience with his wife as she works through her issues of anger. We are all in the process of God changing us from our fallen condition into His glorious image.

Bearing the other instead of focusing on how their sin is affecting us is much easier said than done at times for both spouses; I realize that. But let's not forget that Christians are called to "long-suffer" (the old King James term) with one another.

This was so important for Rose and me to learn. How could we hope to rebuild our marriage if we couldn't bear one another? We had to choose not to focus on how the other's actions were affecting us personally. We had to learn to show compassion to each other and to pray for each other.

I admit that Rose was forced to learn all of this long before I did. I can't tell you how many times I was a jerk to her but remained oblivious to my actions for days. Sooner or later, though, I would dutifully repent to her and Rose would just say, "I know, I've been praying for you." She wasn't spending those days waiting to point out my failures to me. She simply prayed for me. I will tell you that her humble and patient attitude toward me did more to motivate me to be a good husband than anything else could have.

All of this holds just as true for the husband. If a man wants his wife to become more supportive, he should treat her with kindness and patience. Getting impatient with her will only slow down the process.

It may help to remember how Jesus treats you when

you've failed. Does He stand before you with arms crossed, condemning you and accusing you? Or does He wash your feet, pleading for you to draw close to Him in repentance, opening His arms to welcome you back? Beloved, which of these two actions best describes the way you treat your spouse? Do you think God sees you more as an "accuser of the brethren," or more as one who is willing to bear their faults?

We may seldom think in these terms, but there is more at stake than our own happiness, or even our own marriage. The truth is people need to see Christ. Do you recall Doubting Thomas? Although he had the testimony of numerous eyewitnesses, he declared that he would not believe in Jesus' resurrection until he saw Him with his own eyes. So Jesus revealed Himself to Thomas. But He did something particularly noteworthy on that occasion: He pointed out the marks of suffering on His hands and His side. And Thomas was instantly undone. When he saw the proof of Jesus' suffering, he believed. Husbands, Wives, may I say to you that it is still the same today? When people see the marks of suffering in us, they are seeing Jesus. Our response to suffering is an undeniable proof that Jesus lives. It is the one thing that will always separate Christians from imposters or adherents of other religions. Christians don't declare holy war on others; we love them and bear them. "The Christian leaders who shook the world were one and all men of sorrows whose witness to mankind welled out of heavy hearts."[5]

GOD OF ALL COMFORT

There is one more aspect to this business of mourning that we must mention: those who mourn shall be comforted!! What could be more important than having God fill us with His heavenly life and to bring us into union with Himself? We have all been called to be mourners and sufferers with Christ. The consolation is this: when Jesus brings us His Cross, He also brings His presence. Most of the despair and anguish couples experience from marital difficulties results from focusing on their problems rather than on Christ. He knows His own, so He knows how to comfort them. He sometimes uses the very grief of marital problems to bring about a sweetness of peace, a peace which is always just beyond the reach of those who have exempted themselves from sorrow.

From my old life, there is one night which I will never forget. I had been out all night doing my thing, and as I came into our apartment I was expecting a tidal wave of anger from my wife. Unbeknownst to me, however, God had been dealing with Rose's will all night. He had been using her suffering to draw her to Himself. She realized that I could die in my sin and my eternity in hell would be sealed. She somehow got her eyes off of herself, and entered into Jesus' mourning over my soul.

When I walked in, I sensed immediately that something was different. There was an indescribable peace permeating the atmosphere in our apartment. The Lord was present in a powerful way! Rose came out of the bedroom with her face full of the peace of God from praying all night. She looked at me with compassionate eyes and simply said, "I forgive you, now you need to go to God and ask Him to forgive you." She then turned around and went back into the bedroom, closing the door behind her. It would have been much easier if she would have screamed at me. I knew the Lord was doing something very real in her. It just magnified how "out of it" I was, and it set the stage for God to bring me under a deep conviction. The impact God had on me that night would never have come about if Rose would have reacted to me as she had in the past. She was able to respond to me this way because she was experiencing His comfort through her mourning. And in her suffering, I caught a glimpse of Jesus that ultimately changed my life.

God mourns over sin and is moved with compassion to alleviate the one who is under its curse. If we will learn how to mourn and embrace the suffering of Christ, we will come to know His comfort, and then we will be able to share that comfort with others. The minister that married Rose and me shared on our wedding day what we can now see was a prophetic word. He said that many tears would be shed, but that others would benefit from our testimony. Rose and I don't regret one bit of what we have gone through. We know that what we have been through has brought us closer to God and has allowed us to become a channel of His blessings to others. But His blessing isn't reserved for just the two of us. God is inviting you, too, to enter into His suffering. He wants to make your life and marriage a testimony of hope to others, as well. He can only do that if you will embrace a spirit of mourning and suffering. Please don't miss what God wants to give you: Himself.

"The Lord Jesus cannot live in us fully and reveal Himself through us until the proud self within us is broken. This simply means that the hard, unyielding self, which justifies itself, wants its own way, stands up for its rights, and seeks its own glory, at last bows its head to God's will, admits its wrong, gives up its own way to Jesus, surrenders its rights, and discards its own glory—that the Lord Jesus might have all and be all. In other words, it is dying to self and self-attitudes."[1]

~ Roy Hession

Chapter Four

OBEDIENCE TO GOD

"Blessed are the meek, for they shall inherit the earth."
(Matthew 5:5)

*I*t had been several weeks since Katherine had left her husband John. They had only been married for a couple of years when his severe sexual addiction had forced her to pursue a divorce. His addiction to pornography and numerous encounters with prostitutes had been bad enough, but recently he had pressured her to become sexually involved with other couples. She had done her best to hold the marriage together, but the constant pain arising from his enormous desire for other women eventually became too much for her to handle.

Not long after leaving John she met Prince Charming. This man constantly showed her that he understood the value of a good woman. He lavished her with attention and affection. Although the painful ordeal she had just endured made her hesitant to become involved with another man, it also made the attention she was receiving all the more welcome.

Over the next several weeks, Katherine felt herself being swept up into this man's life. Her marriage and her husband seemed but distant memories. The fact that she was happy for the first time in a long time made what she did next entirely unexplainable. One day she was driving down the road when she felt strangely compelled to call her husband. She was surprised to find out that he finally had surrendered his life to Christ. She was genuinely happy for him but any idea of returning to him was absolutely unthinkable. Not only had she lost all of her feelings for him, but she had become convinced that Prince Charming was a gift to her from God.

John and Katherine mostly discussed practical things like tax returns and so on. Suddenly, he announced to her that she should return to him. When she resisted this suggestion, he told her to call her parents about it. She was happy to do this, knowing how furious they were when they found out all that he had put her through. "I'll just make the call and get this over with right now," she thought to herself.

Much to her shock, her father told her unequivocally that she needed to be home with her husband. She had never heard such conviction in her father's voice before. Her mother and sister both got on the phone to support his statement. She was an adult and normally would not allow her family to exert undue influence on her decisions, but she *knew* that this was the Lord speaking to her through them. Once she understood that it was God who was telling her to do this, the argument was over. She knew she had to obey.

However, obeying the voice of God is not always an easy thing to do. Her first reaction at the thought of leaving her boyfriend and returning to her husband caused her overwhelming grief. She collapsed in tears. In spite of how repulsed she was at the thought, outright disobedience to the Lord was not an option for her.

For months she kept her feelings to herself. The fact that John was finally smothering her with love did not help matters. It would have almost been easier if he had been the selfish jerk that she had grown accustomed to. The ordeal of losing her had caused him to fall in love with her, but she continued to feel repulsed by him. She wanted to return to her boyfriend. The only thing that kept her there was the sense that she dare not disobey God.

Over time, the marriage of John Steven and Katherine Ann Gallagher was rebuilt in God's love. Her obedience that day paved the way for the birth of Pure Life Ministries.

Those who do not know the Lord cannot comprehend this kind of blind obedience. The willingness to submit to the will of God—even when everything within the person wants to go his own way—comes about through the process of repentance described in the Beatitudes.

The unbelieving people of this world gain no benefit from experiencing the futility and emptiness of life without God. The sufferings of this world and the sorrows of sin are meaningless to them. But to those who belong to Christ, these painful experiences accomplish a vital purpose: they allow the Lord an ever greater reign over their lives. Poverty of spirit and mourning over one's sinful condition are meant to bring the Christian into a greater submission to the lordship of Jesus Christ.

"Meekness," wrote Rex Andrews, "is submission, voluntarily, to the will of another, in order to patiently obey and do the word of another. It is patient endurance in submission and obedience…This meekness-humility is the humbling and surrender of the will to obedience to the will of God. It is the path of patience and endurance. It is the true bearing of the Cross."[2] That is the best definition and description of meekness I have ever read.

Without first coming to the place of poverty and mourning, we simply cannot submit our wills to God. What Kathy Gallagher did back in 1982 would have been impossible for her had she not already experienced poverty of spirit and godly sorrow over her sin. Until a person really comes to an end of Self and experiences anguish over their sin, they will never know what it means to live in true submission to God. Instead of having their wills swallowed up in His, they will go through life picking and choosing when they will obey the Lord.

Believe me, I know just what I'm asking of you in this journey of restoring your marriage. It has taken me years to apprehend what I'm sharing with you. I don't want to withhold hard truth from you, but neither do I wish to push you to accomplish in a few days what it has taken me years to learn. And hopefully it is understood even without my saying it that I still have much to learn and apply in my marriage. Rose and I are not at the summit of marital bliss, but we do know a thing or two about letting God turn the ashes of what we once had into the ever-increasing beauty of what we now have.

LIVING IN SUBJECTION TO GOD'S AUTHORITY

Fortunately, God isn't asking us to pursue restoration of our marriages without providing the help we need. Thus Jesus calls us to enter into His yoke: "Come unto Me, all ye that labor and are heavy laden, and I will give you rest. Take My yoke upon you and learn of Me; for I am meek and lowly in heart: and ye shall find rest unto your souls. For My yoke is easy, and My burden is light." (Matthew 11:28-30 KJV) In this passage, Jesus reassures those who have experienced the first two beatitudes that they will find rest for their souls by living in submission to His rule. "Take My yoke upon you and learn of Me; for I am meek and lowly in heart," Jesus says. Yoked together with Him we begin to partake of His meekness. And that meekness produces the rest our souls so desperately need.

The pain of infidelity can go very deep into the person who has been wronged. However, failing to respond in God's way only intensifies and prolongs the victim's misery. The wounded wife desperately needs the rest of soul and healing of heart that come about through a submissive union with Christ. Rose and I have encountered plenty of wives who understandably have been devastated by their husband's sexual sin. They seem unable to extend the forgiveness that Christ requires. My heart goes out to them. But I know they are only prolonging what God wants to do for them—lighten their emotional burden and give them comforting rest in the midst of their turmoil. Jesus calms the storms of whatever emotion they may be dealing with and gives peace for weary souls, no matter how high the waves. His peace and rest is unmistakable. I experienced this with Rose as she was learning to yield to God in the midst of our trials. Seeing how she was being buoyed by a supernatural peace actually made me want to respond to God in the same way. When both parties in a marriage meekly submit to God in this way, His Holy Spirit begins to transform and melt their hearts into His. As they enter into His yoke, His cords of love begin to bind their hearts together into one with Him.

Part of the submission process is allowing God's authority to become established in the marital relationship. As Rose and I came back together, we soon realized that our roles had become reversed. Our relationship wasn't in the proper order of God's design for marriage. Such role reversal is becoming the norm in Christian homes but it is all the more prevalent when sexual sin becomes involved. In our case, because I had been in my sin for years, Rose had taken charge of the spiritual, financial, and basic needs of the home. I was pretty much consumed with my sin and consequently had neglected my place as the spiritual head of the home. As our leaders at Pure Life Ministries began to teach us the principles of godly marriage, it became obvious that Rose was carrying a load that God did not design her to carry.

There is no way to avoid saying it: God has ordained the husband to be the head over the wife.* Couples would be wise to heed this Scriptural mandate. Paul clearly defined the role of the husband and wife in Ephesians 5:

---

* I will not attempt to define the roles of husband and wife extensively, for that is not my goal. There are many good, biblically based books that will do that for you, such as, *A Marriage Without Regrets* by Kay Arthur, *The Complete Husband*, by Lou Priolo, or *The Excellent Wife*, by Martha Peace.

Wives, submit to your own husbands, as to the Lord. For the husband is head of the wife, as also Christ is head of the church; and He is the Savior of the body. Therefore, just as the church is subject to Christ, so let the wives be to their own husbands in everything.

Husbands, love your wives, just as Christ also loved the church and gave Himself for her...that He might present her to Himself a glorious church, not having spot or wrinkle or any such thing, but that she should be holy and without blemish. So husbands ought to love their own wives as their own bodies. (Ephesians 5:24-28a)

One of the reasons many wives resist this kind of submission is that they sense their husbands are using their God-given position for selfish purposes. It is normal in the devil's kingdom to rule by force. But people who have been granted authority in the kingdom of God operate under a completely different set of values. They rule by love. Kay Arthur brings this out beautifully in her excellent book, *A Marriage Without Regrets*:

She [Christ's bride] was to be loved even though she was yet unlovely and covered with many spots, wrinkles, and blemishes. Christ loved her to the utmost so that she might blossom into her full beauty, holy and blameless. That's also the prescription for Christian marriages. A husband is to focus on his wife, even though he notices spots and wrinkles and blemishes that he wishes were not there. His role—his sacred calling, his holy task—is to love her until she blossoms into her full beauty as a woman, radiant and stunning as she reflects the very holiness of Christ...If husbands would follow this single rule, it's doubtful any Christian wife would find submission at all distasteful.[3]

Men who have long since relinquished their rightful position as priest of the home need to move forward patiently. For instance, when I finally began to step into my role as the leader of the home, I couldn't just jump onto the wagon and rip the reins out of her hands, and say, "Ok, I'm in charge now!" I owed it to Rose to be considerate of her feelings.

On the wife's side, it is equally important that she submits herself to God's authority structure in the home. She, too, must be patient with her husband as he moves into his role as spiritual leader. This responsibility is new to him and it will take time before he learns to do it right. But Peter makes it very clear that regardless of his mistakes, she must do her utmost to submit to him. He wrote, "Wives, likewise, be submissive to your own husbands, that even if some do not obey the word, they, without a word, may be won by the conduct of their wives, when they observe your chaste conduct accompanied by fear." (I Peter 3:1-2)

The wife needs to realize that the issue isn't her husband's fitness for the position; the issue is God's declaration of how the home should be set up. Submitting to her husband is the tangible proof of her submission to God. The husband, on the other hand, needs to understand his responsibility to gently and lovingly relieve his wife of the burden that he should be carrying.

The need to reverse roles is the situation many couples face when working on restoring their marriage. I knew my home was out of whack, and it was my responsibility, under the leading of the Holy Spirit, to put it in order again. I have to admit, I was quite intimidated at the outset. Rose was clearly a lot further along than me spiritually. And although that is often the case, it doesn't change the biblical mandate. Wives need their husbands to take their proper role.

I remember how one day God allowed me to see that Rose wasn't as strong as I thought she was. She fell apart emotionally before my eyes and I was stabbed in the heart with the sudden realization of all that I had laid upon her. I had allowed the burden of our home to rest on her shoulders. On top of the tremendous daily pressures of working full-time and running a home, she also had to deal with the extra burden of my sin. I finally saw that it was only God's grace that had enabled her to hold up as well as she had; it was now time for me to relieve her.

Many wives of men in sexual sin have had to carry the weight of their homes—dealing with the finances, parenting the children and making the major decisions. Their reluctance to yield these responsibilities to a man who has an established track record of being completely irresponsible is very natural and understandable.

The transition to God's authority structure is a difficult process for every couple, but it is a necessary and vital part of coming under God's authority, both in your own personal walk and in your marriage. It requires a heart of meekness in both the husband and the wife. Meekness is the key that opens the door to submission in a heart.

Something to Light Our Way

There is another important aspect of obedience to God that must be touched on here. It is true that there are times when the Lord directly communicates His will in a given situation, as He did for Kathy Gallagher in the story I shared at the beginning of this chapter. But more often, God's wishes are made known through His Word.

We are told that Scripture is a lamp to our feet and a light to our path. (Psalm 119:105) Not only does the Bible inform us of His will, but as a light on a path of darkness, it shows us how to follow the right way and avoid the wrong way.

Unless the Word of God becomes the absolute standard

by which a couple is led and guided, they will most certainly be led down the wrong pathway. God's Word has all the answers to your problems and is able to accomplish what may seem to be the impossible. I am astounded and grieved when Christians look to books that water down and even go against the principles laid down by God Himself in Scripture. God's children will never experience the fulfillment that comes through a submitted life if they turn to extra-biblical sources for their counsel.

"All Scripture is given by inspiration of God, and is profitable for *doctrine*, for *reproof*, for *correction*, for *instruction in righteousness*, that the man of God *may be complete*, thoroughly equipped for every good work." (II Timothy 3:16-17, emphasis added) This passage of Scripture shows us how God can give us everything we need from His Word. By looking to the Word of God for guidance, couples will find that they will be thoroughly equipped to bring about a complete work in their marriage. I'd like to use the four terms from this verse—doctrine, reproof, correction, instruction—to identify four areas where meekness is a required element of the restoration process.

Doctrine: "I Submit"

The first of the four terms is *doctrine*, which in the Greek root *didaskalia* means *instruction, learning,* or *teaching.* We are basically ignorant when it comes to the things of God and are in desperate need to learn of His ways, His kingdom and His character. We need to be taught the Lord's will, His commandments, pleasures, likes, dislikes, etc. Doctrine is God's way of instructing ignorant man in the things He expects of them. Since the fall of man, sin has corrupted man's perspective.

What I'm about to say may sound too strong to some, but I have realized in my own life that I am literally insane without the Word of God. Human thinking, untempered by God's

Truth, leads to insane thoughts and actions. What else would explain my obsession with crack cocaine, porn and prostitutes? I was acting like a madman! The truth is that there is no limit to the insanity we can indulge in if we choose to operate outside of the truth of God's Word. Praise the Lord for His Word! We are ignorant and blind; desperately needy for instruction in the things of God. A meek person responds to the instruction and teaching—the doctrine—of Scripture by saying, "I submit."

Reproof: "I Am Wrong"

A second way we can profit from God's Word is by *reproof.* In the Greek the term *elegcov* means "to convict," or "to identify error." Because of His great love for us, Jesus is ever ready to identify wrong thinking that is going on within us. "The Word of God is living and powerful, and sharper than any two-edged sword, piercing even to the division of soul and spirit, and of joints and marrow, and is a discerner of the thoughts and intents of the heart. And there is no creature hidden from His sight, but all things are naked and open to the eyes of Him to whom we must give account." (Hebrews 4:12-13) When we allow the Word of God to permeate our thinking, the Holy Spirit is able to point out to us when we get off track in some way. A meek person is quick to admit he or she is wrong.

Consider for a moment the practical working out of the role reversal that needs to occur in the marriage devastated by sexual sin. May I testify plainly that both husband and wife are likely to make some mistakes in that difficult process? A wife may suddenly be overcome by fear or distrust and resist submitting to her husband in some area. The husband may lose his temper, like I did on that trip to get the pickup truck in Tennessee. Both the husband and the wife need a little breathing room to fail. But it is so important to be quick to say, "I'm wrong" when we fail. Rose and I failed on a regular basis through this process so it was vital that we knew how to humble ourselves and acknowledge our mistakes to each other.

God realizes we will fail, so He established in His Word how we ought to respond when we have blown it in some way. God requires repentance. He equates repentance with a "broken spirit and a contrite heart." (Psalm 51:17) Sounds a lot like meekness, doesn't it? Unquestionably the two concepts go hand in hand. That's another reason why it is so essential for couples on the road to restoration to develop an attitude of meekness. They will need to respond to their own mistakes with repentance, and they will need to respond to the mistakes of their spouse with forgiveness. In marriage, many times the solution to a problem is simply to say "I'm wrong, and I repent. Will you please forgive me?" Both repentance and forgiveness, if they are genuine, are rooted in a heart of meekness.

Correction: "I Don't Know"

The third way we can profit from God's Word is through *correction*. In the Greek the word is *epanorywsiv*, meaning a "straightening up again." In layman's terms it is the corrective change that follows repentance. All of us are bent toward sin and need to be straightened out on a regular basis. "Good and upright is the Lord: therefore will He teach sinners in the way. The meek He will guide in judgment: and the meek will He teach His way." (Psalm 25:8-9 KJV) The promise given here that God will teach us and guide us is a conditional promise that is linked to meekness. Meekness is the attitude which invites God to correct us and teach us. God can't work in a proud or self-willed person. A person who is in that state won't respond to God's reproof. The Lord will first have to work on breaking down a stiff-necked person through various situations and consequences. As you are no doubt learning, sometimes He chooses to use a problematic marriage. He is willing to do whatever it takes to help us. He realizes more than we do just how crucial it is to teach meekness to sinners so that they can turn and obey His Word.

It is absolutely vital that Christian couples remain teachable. The only way that happens is for each spouse to be quick to acknowledge, "I don't know." This requires a great deal of humbling.

Rose and I knew our home was out of order because it didn't line up with the Word of God. We knew that things had to change to bring our home and our marriage into God's established pattern. We had to be willing to look into His Word for instruction on what our proper roles and responses toward one another should be. For many couples, this will also involve a willingness to seek outside help. It took the intervention of Pure Life Ministries for Rose and me to bring our marriage, our home, and our lives into alignment with God's Word. We might not have made it had we not received such strong guidance from our mentors at the ministry.

Discipline: "I'll Do It"

Lastly, God's Word is profitable for *instruction in righteousness.* The term instruction here is the Greek word, *paideia,* meaning to "train; by implication, through practice and discipline." A meek person doesn't just agree with God, he goes and does what He commands. You have to respond on a daily basis and be a doer of the word to profit by it. It's hard; it takes work and consistency. Just like an athlete who trains, a follower of Christ must also train daily in the things pertaining to His Word. "A disciple is not above his teacher, but everyone who is perfectly trained will be like his teacher." (Luke 6:40)

A couple has to realize that learning and living the Word of God will be a lifetime endeavor. Every day provides an opportunity for each spouse to either yield to God in their attitudes and actions, or to resist Him. In the day-in, day-out course of life these opportunities can be very subtle.

Just the other day, I had one of those opportunities. I had

just gotten out of bed when Rose informed me that I needed to move something upstairs. I quickly muttered, "Yeah, yeah; not now." In other words, "Don't you see I just rolled out of bed? Why are you bothering me with such trivial things now?" I walked out of the bedroom and headed downstairs to have my prayer time. As I sat there in my chair, doing my utmost to enter into communion with the Lord, the Holy Spirit said, "You're wrong; you need to go and repent to your wife." I had a choice. I could meekly yield to God, or I could stubbornly dig my heels in and refuse. I relented and said, "Yes Lord. I'll do it." So, I went back to the bedroom and gave my wife a kiss on the cheek and said "You know what, I'm just wrong; I'm sorry, and I love you." Whatever tension there was immediately lifted and I could sense God's love and peace in our midst.

I can't tell you how many times we both have gone to one another and repented like this. We are determined not to give place to the devil in our marriage. We are very aware that he is always seeking to drive a wedge between us. But when the prevailing atmosphere of the home is one of humility and meekness, quarrels, disagreements, tension, anger or any other kind of evil will fail to thrive. The devil can't get a foothold when two people are willing to repent to one another. I could hardly over-emphasize how important it is to practice doing the right thing toward one another. These four simple phrases have a great deal to do with what God has been able to do in our marriage.

- "I submit."
- "I am wrong."
- "I don't know."
- "I'll do it."

Speak these words often; live with the spiritual realities they represent; submit yourself to God's structure of authority and you will soon see the fruit of a godly and fulfilling marriage!

Miracle Marriage Number Two

TOM AND SUE

*A*fter months of preparation and planning, the big day finally arrived on August 10, 1996. Tom and Sue were prominent singles in the large church they went to, assuring that their wedding would be well attended. It should have been one of the most joyous days of their lives, but Tom was struggling with a fear unknown to Sue: he was greatly concerned about whether or not he could actually love his new wife in the way he had just expressed in his vows.

Unbeknownst to anyone in that reception hall, Tom had a long history of viewing pornography and having sexual encounters with other men. "I entered into marriage deceitful to my wife and delusional about the seriousness of my addiction," Tom remembers with a grimace.

For better or worse, the newlyweds were soon off on their honeymoon. A week later they returned home and went about making their new life together. Unfortunately, it wasn't long before the old temptations started plaguing Tom again. One day he gave in, opening the floodgates of sin back into his life. He started visiting adult bookstores and viewing pornography online. His secret sex life also destroyed any natural desire to be intimate with his wife.

Sue was clueless about his sexual sin but instinctively knew that something was terribly wrong in their relationship. "For the first five years of our marriage, I struggled to figure out what was the 'virus' eating away at our marriage. What was it about me that drove Tom away from me? What more could I possibly do to make him love me? Why wasn't our marriage like those that other people have?"

Tom dealt with his guilt by helping Sue around the house. In that regard, he was an exceptional husband. "Thinking back, it was as if I had this set of scales in my mind. I convinced myself that doing household chores somehow made up for my secret sin."

Occasionally, Sue would attempt to confront Tom about his aloofness and lack of interest in her. He would always promise to do better, but before long the relationship would fall back into the same predictable rut. One Saturday in particular Sue pleaded with him to tell her what was wrong. He just downplayed the whole thing and offered his usual list of promises.

"To be honest, we didn't have much of a marriage," Tom admits. "Everyone at the church thought we did, however. We were careful to never argue in front of others. In fact, because we were so involved in church activities, people tended to see us as the perfect couple. If hidden cameras had been set up in our home, a different story would have come out. We basically lived our lives as roommates."

Even though she was clearly a victim of her husband's deception, Sue had her own issues as well. "Our marriage was draining me emotionally, but I was too prideful to seek counseling. I didn't want others to know that our marriage was a wreck."

In the fall of 2000, Tom was caught looking at pornography on a church computer. He made a partial confession of his problem—hiding his involvement with men and minimizing the extent of his porn addiction. He promised that he would never do it again and the optimistic church leaders paired him up with an accountability partner as part of his "restoration process." Tom met with the man on a regular basis but never admitted to anything other than occasional lust.

It would be another two-and-a-half painful years before the truth really came out about Tom's secret life. This time he admitted everything, even confessing his sin in front of the church during a Sunday evening service. "I actually was relieved," he now says. "It was terribly embarrassing, but at least I didn't have to hide anymore. I could finally tell the truth about my sin issues."

That week he showed up at Pure Life Ministries (PLM). Although his wife had a lot of anger about the things he had done, Sue decided from the beginning that she was going to stand beside Tom through the process. She decided to enter the telephone counseling program while he was at PLM.

"It became obvious to us that to put our marriage back together, God had to put us, as individuals, back together," Tom says. "There were layers of selfishness and sin in both of us that God had to expose. I had years of blatant sin to repent of and work through. Sue had to deal with anger and bitterness over my sin, deceptiveness and lack of love."

"I was relieved that Tom went to PLM and hopeful that our marriage might be different, Sue recalls. "But I was also angry about how far things had gone. I had never heard of Pure Life Ministries and I was somewhat fearful of what kind of place he was going to. All my fears were alleviated the first time I visited him there."

The roller coaster of emotions between hatred and love for Tom continued on for the first few months. But over time Sue's heart began to soften. Her change of attitude actually had more to do with what the Lord was showing her about herself than it did about how Tom was doing. "When the Lord began to reveal the ugliness that was inside *my heart*, my perspective of Tom's sin began to change."

Tom did very well in the Live-In program. He really found the Lord in a powerful new way. Like Sue, it happened as he began to see the reality of his sin: how much it affected his wife, the Lord and other people. "Little by little the cloud was lifting off of my heart. All I had seen for years was darkness. As truth was poured into my soul at Pure Life, God began to change me."

One benefit that has come out of this painful process has been a brand new marriage. "We didn't receive a list of ten things to improve our marriage that we had to do and check off every day," Tom says. "We were taught to get our focus on Jesus Christ. As we learned to love Him, our attitudes completely changed toward each other and toward life in general."

"Sometimes, in my more contemplative moments, I am amazed at what God has done in such a short time. Sue is simply a different person. Sometimes I marvel at the things she wants to do. In fact, sometimes it downright overwhelms me! She serves now because she has a deeper sense of what God has done for her. When she packs a lunch or babysits or homeschools or counsels or volunteers, it is done because she loves Christ. God has changed her. He has changed us."

"It was no mistake that I became Tom's wife," Sue adds. "The trials I have gone through have brought me into a real relationship with the Lord."

"We are so thankful for what He has done and is continuing to do. A hymn we sang at our wedding which had little meaning to me at the time rings so much deeper and truer now: 'To God be the glory. Great Things He hath done.'"

*"Sanctification is about our own choices
and behavior. It involves work. Empowered
by God's Spirit, we strive. We fight sin.
We study Scripture and pray,
even when we don't feel like it.
We flee temptation. We press on; we run
hard in the pursuit of holiness. And as we become
more and more sanctified, the power of the gospel
conforms us more and more closely,
with ever-increasing clarity,
to the image of Jesus Christ."*[1]

~ C. J. Mahaney

Chapter Five

SEEKERS AFTER HIS RIGHTEOUSNESS

*"Blessed are those who hunger and thirst for righteousness,
for they shall be filled."* (Matthew 5:6)

arcus and Linda Jones were typical Christian parents. Five children in the home guaranteed a hectic schedule! School and church activities kept the family in a constant mode of movement. And yet, there always seemed to be time for television.

Friday evenings became the high spot of every week. The family would gather around the large screen TV to watch that week's designated movie. Marcus and Linda would cringe a little when inappropriate scenes were shown in the PG-13 and R-rated movies they watched, but not enough to stop the practice. "I would rather my kids were at home watching a movie with a little flesh or violence than to be out on the streets doing who-knows-what," they would tell each other.

The truth is that Linda did her utmost to be a good mom. She also had a genuine desire to lead each of her children to the Lord. "We had this idea in our minds that we needed to entertain our kids and their friends into wanting Jesus," she recalls. "So we took them to all kinds of youth events, concerts, game nights, movie nights and so on. Looking back on it now I can see that there was very little of God's presence in any of it."

Such was life in the Jones household until the truth came out that Marcus had been unfaithful to Linda. In one terrible afternoon, life as she had known it was completely overturned. As the two attempted to pick up the pieces of their marriage, they turned to Pure Life Ministries for help. "Up until that point, you could not have told me that there was anything wrong in our home," says Linda. "In fact, I would have told you that we had a godly home. Looking back now, I can see how superficial my perspectives were about Christianity."

One of the first things that became painfully evident to both of them was the fact that they were far more interested in worldly entertainment than they were spiritual things. "I even remember the Tuesday night Bible studies we held in our home with some of the other folks from the church," Marcus states. "As soon as the study was over we would turn on our TV to catch the end of 'American Idol' to see who would be booted off that week!"

One of the highlights of their time in the Overcomers At-Home program was when they read Steve Gallagher's book, *Intoxicated with Babylon*. "Oh my gosh," Linda says, shaking her head. "I just had no idea how I had allowed our home to become corrupted by the spirit of the world. That book alone completely changed the atmosphere of our home."

Part of that change happened when they put their television up for sale. One of the kids asked them if they were becoming Amish. Another exclaimed, "Now I know Mom has gone off the deep end!"

Instead of coming home from school and finding Mom watching the "Oprah Winfrey Show," they would find her sitting in her chair reading the Word of God. After dinner they saw Dad doing his Bible study instead of watching "Survivor." Things took a radical new course in the Jones home. It took a while for the kids to get used to the new lifestyle, but over time they came to accept it and even respect their parents for standing by their new convictions. In short, Jesus replaced entertainment as the center of the Jones household.

There is a vacuum that takes place within any person who starts down the path laid out in the Beatitudes. The sincere seeker discovers an entire new realm opened up to him as the pursuit of idolatry and sin dies off. He now finds his attention turning to the spiritual realm and the central Figure of that realm: Jesus Christ. A new passion to know Him and draw close to Him emerges within his heart. Somehow, in the midst of seeking His face, His righteousness is imputed into the believer's life.

The subject of this book is marriage, of course. But it needs to be said that having a healthy marriage comes about as a result of being focused on issues of even more importance. A good marital relationship is one of the many blessings that come about when people put God in His rightful place in their lives. "But seek first the kingdom of God and His righteousness, and all these things shall be added to you," Jesus said. (Matthew 6:33) There is no adding on of "these things" in your marriage until both husband and wife are unified in seeking His kingdom and righteousness.

Seeking God and His righteousness must be one of the primary focuses of life. This pursuit of God isn't meant to be a means to an end but the end itself. The Psalms portray this passion frequently:

- As for me, I will see Your face in righteousness; I shall be satisfied when I awake in Your likeness. (Psalm 17:15)

- God, You are my God; early will I seek You; my soul thirsts for You; my flesh longs for You in a dry and thirsty land where there is no water. (Psalm 63:1)

- As the deer pants for the water brooks, so pants my soul for You, O God. My soul thirsts for God, for the living God. (Psalm 42:1-2a)

- I spread out my hands to You; my soul longs for You like a thirsty land. (Psalm 143:6)

I'm painting the picture for you of where you are headed. I know you probably feel like you're a great way off from this place now. But do not lose heart; God *is* taking you there. And as you progress in developing poverty of spirit, embracing the spirit of mourning, and surrendering in meekness, the automatic response of hungering and thirsting for righteousness will well up in you. You won't have to work hard to initiate it, nor will you have to fake it. These metaphors of hungering and thirsting describe involuntary human drives. Hungering and thirsting for righteousness "hurts; it is painful; it is like actual, physical hunger and thirst," writes Martyn Lloyd-Jones. "It is something that goes on increasing and makes one feel desperate. It's something that causes suffering and agony [when the need goes unmet]."[2]

A Radical Response to a Radical Call

As God was calling Rose and me down a deeper path with Him, this hunger I am describing to you led to our decision to leave New York and move to Kentucky. All we knew at this point was that we needed and wanted more of God. The Lord was beckoning us to give Him everything so He could have sole possession of us. He was leading us into the wilderness where He could dry up everything we had been looking to for fulfillment outside of Him. Even though there were still issues from our past, we knew the solution wasn't to look back, but to move forward in the things of God. Our marriage wasn't the focus; it was Him. We knew this new commitment meant that everything about our lives in this world had to change.

Being open to drastic change is a very important factor for the couple who desires God to work in their marriage; especially when sexual sin has been involved. Yet it is a point where many couples err. Some are anxious to get back to the old lifestyle minus only the sexual sin. They miss the fact that the Lord is calling them unto Himself. This can mean making a move, changing careers, downsizing a home, or any number of things. We were called to give our lives in full-time ministry but that may not be what God calls you to. Nevertheless, He is definitely calling you into a deeper relationship with Himself. Are you listening to His call? Are you heeding His direction?

The great call on our lives wasn't to work for Pure Life Ministries; it was to enter into a deeper life in God. It quickly became obvious how much we were being controlled by the spirit of this world. Our culture is inundated with a corrupting spirit which daily pours in upon the believer's mind through movies, television, advertising, magazines, the Internet and the music industry. In his book, *Intoxicated with Babylon*, Steve Gallagher systematically exposes this spirit, detailing how it has infiltrated the Church and is seducing God's people in these last days. The Bible, in the original Greek language, uses the term *kosmos* to identify the spirit of this world. "*Kosmos*," Steve writes, "is constantly seeking to transfer its repulsive and diabolical mindset onto believers. Any believer who lends his ear to the voice of *kosmos* is going to be affected by it. We have to remember that the spirit of the world appeals to the desires of our lower nature. The pull exerted by those lusts should never be underestimated. The enemy knows how to lure believers into his camp by catering to those ungodly passions."[3]

Like Marcus and Linda, Steve's book opened our eyes to what was happening around us. God was calling us to separate ourselves from the allurements and influences of the world. But Steve Gallagher isn't the only minister who has written about the effects of worldliness. In his epic work, *Studies in the Sermon on the Mount*, Martyn Lloyd-Jones writes: "The man we have been looking at in terms of these Beatitudes is a man who has come to see that the world in which he lives is controlled by sin and Satan; he sees that he is under the control of a malign influence, he has been walking 'according to the prince of the power of the air, the spirit that now worketh in the children of disobedience.' He sees that 'the god of this world' has been blinding him to various things, and now he longs to be free from it."[4]

One thing Rose and I had to do was to take an honest look at our home. We had to decide whether or not we were allowing worldly interests to rob us of our time with God. We had to get rid of some things that were allowing the spirit of this world to gain a foothold in our home. Coming to work at Pure Life Ministries helped us in many ways, such as getting rid of our television (since it wasn't allowed), but we still had to do our own housecleaning if we were going to draw close to God.

In those early days we began to see how the god of this world had quenched our hunger for the things of God. Magazines, videos and secular music were all hindrances to a godly atmosphere; it all went into the trash can. Now the way was cleared for us to find the Lord in a very real and powerful way!

SOAKING IN THE WORD OF GOD

Rose and I had spent many years being indoctrinated in the world's thinking. No wonder our marriage was so laden with selfishness! We were being inundated with that worldly "me first" mindset. We desperately needed our minds molded and conformed to God's ways and perspectives. Like most people who come to PLM for help, our devotional life was very meager. During our time in counseling we were required to institute a consistent devotional life first thing in the morning. This daily time grew longer when we came on staff and we had to spend at least two hours every morning seeking the Lord. After that, the staff would come together for yet another hour of prayer or Bible reading.

One of the real blessings that came out of this time of "forced feeding" was how much we came to look forward to our time with the Lord! It was difficult establishing the habit, but over time it became increasingly easier. The more time we spent in the Word, the more we wanted to be in it. That's the way it works. One thing that helped me early on was pray-reading over Psalm 119 every day. Even though the things being expressed there weren't real in my own life, I would ask the Lord to make them real. The Word of God has the power to alter the way you see things. The fact of the matter is that I see things right when I am daily saturating my mind in God's Word. When I'm not putting my heart into my Bible study time, I notice that I am much more susceptible to being led by my emotions or my earthly logic. No wonder so many couples get led astray!

Allow God to make you a hungry Bible reader. Did you catch that? *Allow God.* It means you have a decision to make. God wants to bless you, but you have to be willing to be made hungry.

CLOSET CONVERSATIONS

It probably won't surprise you to hear me say that we need to combine our Bible time with earnest prayer and quiet time spent before God. It may seem like I'm stating the obvious, but I really cannot emphasize this enough because it is so vital to the survival of any kind of spiritual life in God.

I don't know any other way to make my point, so let me write it in bold, capital letters, **PRAYER! PRAYER! PRAYER!** Prayer changes things; and just as importantly, prayer changes you. Rose and I have made a lot of progress, both as individuals and as a married couple. But let me tell you plainly, if we drift into prayerlessness, all of that amazing progress and restoration will collapse. Our lives would quickly dry up. A life in God is the only way out of sin, and it is the only way for God to heal and restore a marriage.

Dear ones, you must understand that the devil is constantly seeking ways to drive a wedge between you and your spouse. He is bent on causing division and strife. How many arguments happen simply because the enemy is somehow able to plant suspicions or the sense of being wronged in one's mind? We stand shell-shocked after a big fight, wondering what in the world just happened. How could we have become so aggravated with one another so soon after affirming our commitment to love and bear one another before God, no matter what?

The problem is we don't do what Jesus said: "Watch and pray, lest you enter into temptation. The spirit indeed is willing, but the flesh is weak." (Mark 14:38) When we aren't praying, we are relying on our own strength to get by. You and I can't withstand a tidal wave of evil if we aren't praying. Martin Luther said, "If I fail to spend two hours in prayer each morning, the devil gets the victory through the day."[5] Hasn't the enemy caused enough defeat in your marriage? The couple who kneels to God in prayer can stand up to anything!

Of course, the most important aspect to prayer is that it brings us into intimacy with God. Do you know how dearly God wants intimacy with you? When I think of how unfaithful I have been to the Lord, it is amazing to me that He still wants to be intimate with me. God yearns for us to come away with Him into sweet fellowship and communion. He is always calling us to His inner chamber. He is always knocking on the door of our hearts wanting access. Won't you let Him in?

When you love and worship something it takes priority and becomes the thing that you make time for, make sacrifices for, and long to be involved in. That has been the driving force in my life of victory over sin. Nothing will keep you from sin like an intimate love affair with God.

The more time each spouse devotes to Jesus in this way, the more each will become like Him. "Make God the center [love] of your heart, the one object of your desire, and prayer will be a blessed fellowship with God. Close and continued fellowship with God will in due time leave its mark and manifest itself to those around us. Just as Moses did not know that his face shone, we ourselves will be unaware of the light of God shining from us."[6] It won't be you *trying* to be a better husband, or you *trying* to be a better wife. Being a better spouse will be the natural outflow of your relationship with God.

SUPPLEMENTING YOUR WALK

A strong devotional life is the most important element in the pursuit of God and His righteousness, but there are also other things couples should do as well. Fellowshipping with like-minded believers is a huge encouragement. I can't tell you what a blessing it is to work at a place where it is the norm to be hungry for God. The Word of God exhorts us to "consider one another in order to stir up love and good works, not forsaking the assembling of ourselves together, as is the manner of some, but exhorting one another, and so much the more as you see the Day approaching." (Hebrews 10:24-25) The book of Acts describes the kind of life the believers of the Early Church lived. Luke wrote, "They continued steadfastly in the apostles' doctrine and fellowship, in the breaking of bread, and in prayers." (Acts 2:42)

Your choice of friends is enormously important. If you hang around people who aren't hungering to know God in a real way, you will find your passion for God being quenched. "Do not be deceived," Scripture warns, "evil company corrupts good habits." (I Corinthians 15:33) Find like-minded believers who will encourage you to seek the Lord.

One of the real sources of grief to me is hearing how many men have returned home after completing the residential program at Pure Life Ministries and are ridiculed about their level of consecration by their old friends from church. One brother called me recently in tears after his Christian friends gave him a hard time because he wouldn't go to the jazz clubs and R-rated movies like he used to do in the past. They accused him of having a holier-than-thou attitude. He asked me in tears, "Do I?" Because I knew him so well, I was able to assure him that he wasn't in a self-righteous spirit. I simply encouraged him to find new friends who really did love the Lord.

People's words can have a powerful effect on a believer's decision. Another source of great sorrow to Rose and me are the many marriages we have seen destroyed by carnal family members. We have dealt with too many wives who were negatively influenced by family and friends telling them what they should do about their marriage situation. At the first sign of trouble, these people will tell a wife things like, "Just leave him;" "God has someone better for you;" or "You don't deserve this." People with a carnal perspective are not the ones a hurting wife needs input from. She needs to be around those who understand what it means to love someone with God's love.

There are many godly people out there who have a passion and hunger for God. Find them—they'll be looking for you too—and make them your friends. It is always an encouragement to meet people who love God in a real way, who are willing to forsake everything else for Him, and who are not willing to compromise their spiritual lives for what this world offers them.

Another great tool that can be used to fuel a passion for the Lord is to read biographies about spiritual leaders from the past. Reading stories of saints like Amy Carmichael, Hudson Taylor and others like them can do a great deal to ignite the passion within you to follow God in the same way. Biographies like these help to promote the right perspective of our lives in this world and what it means to sell out for God. I can't tell you how many times we've heard a wife or a husband comment on how much they were affected by the stories of missionaries included in *The Walk of Repentance*. Similarly, it's not at all uncommon for Rose and me to lie in bed at night and share with one another how a book we are reading is affecting us spiritually.

All these things we have been discussing will promote a hunger for God. The truth is that the Lord is the One who supplies that passion within a believer and yet, if the person doesn't fight to know God in a greater way, that passion will never come forth. It is one of the great mysteries of the kingdom of God. It's what Paul meant when he wrote, "...work out your own salvation with fear and trembling; for it is God who works in you both to will and to do for His good pleasure." (Philippians 2:12b-13) We have our part in the process and the Lord has His.

Beloved, Be Filled!

Jesus invites the thirsty to come to Him and to drink. He entreats us to ask, to seek and to knock with the assurance that it will be opened up to us. "Blessed are you who hunger and thirst after righteousness: for you shall be filled." What will you be filled with? With all the fullness of God. He is the beginning and the end of all things. He is love, in all of its fullness, purity and perfection. To be filled with Him is to know true satisfaction that can be found nowhere else. It is what we were created for.

Too many times we look to one another for fulfillment; this is especially true in marriage. If you make a relationship with a person the primary focus of your life, you will be sorely disappointed. Spurgeon once said, "Our foolish way is to desire, and then set to work to compass what we desire. We do not go to work in God's way, which is to seek Him first, and then expect all things to be added unto us. If we will let our heart be filled with God till it runs over with delight, then the Lord Himself will take care that we shall not want any good thing."[7] Contrary to popular, and may I add, unbiblical notions, only Jesus can fill our so-called "love tank." As each spouse is filled with Him, the love that *He is* will overflow into one another. It will take nothing less than both spouses being filled with all the fullness of God to bring their marriage to a place of completeness in Him.

I can't tell you how many times Rose and I have said to one another, "I never imagined it could be this way." He has given us a reality of Himself, a love for one another and hearts set on eternity. What He has done supersedes anything we could have hoped for. Now, with hindsight, we can see that all we went through was meant to draw us into a deeper walk with Him.

Learn to hunger and thirst for God alone and you will discover the blessedness of being filled with righteousness, in your own personal walk and in your marriage.

*"MERCY is God's supply system
for every need everywhere. Mercy is that kindness,
compassion and tenderness which is a passion to suffer with,
or participate in, another's ills or evils in order to relieve, heal
and restore. It accepts another freely and gladly
AS he is and supplies the needed good of life
to build up and to bring to peace and keep in peace.
It is to take another into one's heart JUST AS HE IS
and cherish and nourish him there.
Mercy takes another's sins and evils and faults
as its own, and frees the other by bearing them to God.
This is the Glow-of-love.
This is the ANOINTING."*[1]

~ Rex B. Andrews

Chapter Six

An Atmosphere of Mercy

"Blessed are the merciful, for they shall obtain mercy."
(Matthew 5:7)

*A*rt had been in the Pure Life Ministries Live-In Program just over a month. He had been involved in sexual sin for nearly thirty years by the time he came to us for help. Despite his twenty years of marriage to Sheila, Art had pursued numerous affairs and encounters with prostitutes. In fact, from the very beginning his relationship with his wife had been laced with deception and manipulation.

One would think that at this point his primary concern would be his wife's feelings, but just the opposite seemed to be the case. He had had a difficult telephone conversation with Sheila just the evening before. He described the tension between them as he saw it, seemingly oblivious to how fresh the wounds were for his wife. In his mind, the past four weeks must have seemed like a year. As he concluded his description of their predicament, I told him about a statement his wife had made to me recently indicating that she didn't feel as though he had been truly broken over his sin.

In response, he proceeded to chronicle a list of sacrifices he had made to leave everything behind and come to Kentucky. He wondered why his wife couldn't at least give him some recognition for how hard it had been for him to come here. In our counseling session, I helped him to see that all he was thinking about was himself, and then bluntly suggested that maybe his wife was right about him not being truly broken.

This man's attitude wasn't unusual. Like many who arrive at PLM, he was neglecting to see how merciful God had been with him. The truth is that he could have easily been abandoned to die in his sins. Not only did he lack gratitude to the Lord, but his self-centered attitude was completely oblivious to what his wife was facing. While he was in a spiritual haven seeking the Lord, she was stuck at home dealing with the bills and everything else associated with the mess that he had made. Had Art truly been in sight of God's mercy to him, he would have been seeking to relieve his wife's burden instead of adding to it.

The good news is that Art did ultimately come to his senses and acknowledge his selfishness. I encouraged him to start focusing on the things he should be grateful for instead of dwelling on how hard he had had it. I reminded him of the importance of being very aware of God's merciful dealings with him. Through our counseling Art also came to grow in his gratitude for Sheila. One of the homework assignments I gave him was to make a list of fifty things about his wife that he was thankful for. This assignment was one of the things the Lord used to help change his attitude. When he started focusing on the way she was willing to stick it out with him after all that he had done, his hardened, selfish heart melted. A new love sprang forth that day that has grown significantly since then. Through his time at PLM, Art received a true revelation of God's mercy that he will never forget.

"Go and learn what this means," Jesus told the group of Pharisees who questioned His dealings with sinners. "I desire mercy and not sacrifice." (Matthew 9:13) Jesus was using this direct quotation from the Old Testament prophets to reveal the heart of God to these religious leaders. Their idea of religion was the scrupulous keeping of rituals and ceremonies. But Jesus was trying to show them that God's heart is one of compassion. This commandment to learn about mercy is just as relevant to us today as it was to those First Century Pharisees.

I told you in an earlier chapter that marriage unites two sinners. On our best days we are still sinners. We husbands will still sin against our wives, and our wives will still sin against us. We can learn a lot about how to deal with one another if we will accept Jesus' invitation to learn about mercy.

In the Old Testament, *mercy* is the English translation of the Hebrew word *hhesed*. English translators utilize three main synonyms to capture the meaning of this potent Hebrew concept: mercy, lovingkindness and kindness. In the fifth beatitude, "Blessed are the merciful, for they shall obtain mercy," the Greek word for "merciful" is *eleemon*. This term represents the essence of what God is, and what He expresses to all mankind through His Son, Jesus Christ. It is what all of us desperately need. Without the mercy of God we would all perish and die in our sins. It is the one common thing that we all possess after coming into the saving grace of the Cross. The poor in spirit, the mourner, the meek, and the one who hungers and thirsts for righteousness all find the relief, the healing, and the needed good of life in the atmosphere of His mercy. "The Lord is gracious and full of compassion, slow to anger and great in mercy. The Lord is good to all, and His tender mercies are over all His works." (Psalm 145:8-9)

At the beginning of this chapter I included the definition of mercy which Rex Andrews penned. I believe this definition provides a full description of the heart of God and merits pondering.

The truth is that we have all committed spiritual adultery against the Lord. We have resisted His loving overtures, rebelled against His authority and done our utmost to live our lives without His interference. And what has the Lord's response been to such utter ingratitude? Like the biblical story of Hosea,

God is relentlessly trying to win us over. Despite our constant rejection, He is ever hopeful of reconciling us with Himself. In short, He has patiently persisted in trying to win our hearts and draw us into a love relationship with Himself.

Very few people ever wake up to the reality of what the Lord has done. Just think of it. God looked down on a world full of harlots and out of it chose a bride for Himself. He knew fully what He was getting. I have often thought of poor Rose on our wedding day: If she really knew what she was getting at the time, she would have run the other direction as fast as her feet could carry her! But when God looked at us, He was very aware of the fact that He would face years of rejection; He was aware that we would flaunt our idols and other loves before Him; and He recognized beforehand that our hearts were prone to stray. Yet He offered us His hand in marriage anyway. He made Himself totally vulnerable, knowing His heart will be trampled over and over again.

MERCY IN THE MARRIAGE

Even with so brief an examination of what the Bible teaches about mercy, it should be readily apparent that we are all rich in mercy. God has given all of us pockets full of mercy. Like the talents given to the master's servants in Jesus' parable of the talents, we too have been given mercy-talents that God expects us to do business with. (see Matthew 25:14-30) He has the right to ask us to be merciful to others in the same way He has been merciful to us. However, it is amazing how stingy we can be with the mercy God has lavished on us. So often we're like the unprofitable servant who buried his mercy-talent in the ground.

In marriage, we quite often feel as though we have to put up with more than should be expected of us. Wives who have been victimized by their husband's sexual sin can easily give way to such feelings. I can remember Rose going through the pain and rejection of my sin, feeling like she had had enough and just wanting to move on with her life. Even though she felt that way, God was telling her to bear me, to pray for me and to forgive me. It was probably the hardest thing she has ever had to do. First of all, a wife in this position looks like a sucker to those who don't understand God's ways. They feel like a doormat, being trampled on over and over again and repeatedly smeared with somebody else's muck. They often wonder why they're allowing this mistreatment to go on. The only answer my wife could give is that God was telling her to. She remembered what God had brought her out of, and she was holding on to the fact that He could do the same for me. No one can respond to such abuse in that spirit unless they have really come to understand and appreciate the mercy that God has done to them.

I know for Rose it would have been easy to lose sight of God's mercy amidst all she was enduring. Fortunately she was going after God and being faithful to Him while I was in my sin. Had she not stayed in sight of the mercy God had done and was doing to her, there would have been a lot less mercy coming my way.

I, too, was susceptible to being unmerciful. It is amazing how some men can twist this marvelous truth about God's mercy around to benefit themselves. When their wives go through the predictable phases of anger and suspicion which result from the way they have been treated, these husbands accuse their wives of being unmerciful. I don't think they are in any position to make such claims!

For me, and I think for most husbands, the hardest thing is simply bearing our wives and allowing them to go through the process of healing. Enduring this is difficult because our wives sometimes "throw-up" on us emotionally. In addition, it's challenging to avoid becoming defensive when our wives express fear or mistrust. In the beginning of the process, I tended to be very defensive if I felt like Rose was being suspicious about my behavior. More than once I responded in anger, and then even if she said she was sorry I would hold it against her. There was something in me that wanted to induce guilt in Rose for not trusting me like I thought she should. And truth be told, sometimes I just didn't want to deal with all of the issues that a husband and wife have to deal with. Marriage demands a lot of forbearance on the part of one another.

PARABLE OF THE UNMERCIFUL HEART

Going through the process of restoring a marriage damaged by sexual sin will quickly expose just how stingy you can be with God's mercy. Unless you are determined to give what has been given to you, the atmosphere of your home won't be an atmosphere of mercy; instead it will be a self-imposed prison of misery.

Jesus brought out the importance of mercy one day when Peter asked him how far believers must go in their forgiveness toward those who have sinned against them: "Lord, how often shall my brother sin against me, and I forgive him? Up to seven times?" Peter thought he was being rather magnanimous with mercy. But Jesus answered: "I do not say to you, up to seven times, but up to seventy times seven." (Matthew 18: 21-22) In other words, there is no limit on mercy. When we are confronted with a situation where mercy is needed, we are expected to extend it freely and without measure.

Immediately following this exchange with Peter, Jesus proceeded to describe how the economy of the kingdom of heaven works.

Therefore the kingdom of heaven is like a certain king who wanted to settle accounts with his servants. And when he had begun to settle accounts, one was brought to him who owed him ten thousand talents. But as he was not able to pay, his master commanded that he be sold, with his wife and children and all that he had, and that payment be made. The servant therefore fell down before him, saying, "Master, have patience with me, and I will pay you all." Then the master of that servant was moved with compassion, released him, and forgave him the debt. (Matthew 18:23-27)

That is exactly what all of us have received who have come to repentance at the foot of the Cross. So imagine, after freely receiving the mercy of God in that way, responding as the servant in this parable responded:

But that servant went out and found one of his fellow servants who owed him a hundred denarii; and he laid hands on him and took him by the throat, saying, "Pay me what you owe!" So his fellow servant fell down at his feet and begged him, saying, "Have patience with me, and I will pay you all." And he would not, but went and threw him into prison till he should pay the debt. (Matthew 18:28-30)

We read this and say to ourselves, "How could he behave so cruelly toward his fellow servant after the mercy he had just received?" Yet we can be the same way, especially in our marriages. I have seen this played out too many times in counseling settings over the years: couples strangling each other, holding on to grudges, keeping a list of wrongs and demanding payment from the other. Jesus went on to show the consequences of such an attitude.

So when his fellow servants saw what had been done, they were very grieved, and came and told their master all that had been done. Then his master, after he had called him, said to him, "You wicked servant! I forgave you all that debt because you begged me. Should you not also have had compassion on your fellow servant, just as I had pity on you?" And his master was angry, and delivered him to the torturers until he should pay all that was due to him. "So My heavenly Father also will do to you if each of you, from his heart, does not forgive his brother his trespasses." (Matthew 18:31-35)

The person, who refuses to give out the mercy that has been given to him, is bound up in a self-imposed prison that can only be unlocked from the inside. What the person with an unmerciful heart never seems to realize is that he is cutting himself off from the very mercy he himself needs.

Sadly, I have seen this scenario played out too often in the life of wives who, after true repentance has occurred in their husband, find it hard to release him from his debt.

I talked to a man the other day who completed the Pure Life Ministries Live-In Program a number of years ago. This man has been faithful to the Lord and to his wife during this entire time. Despite the change in her husband, his wife had proceeded with her plans to divorce him. In spite of this, he determined to love her and to help her in any way he could. He has consistently served her, prayed for her and taken responsibility for the financial needs of the home by working two jobs. Because of an ongoing illness she has had, he has even done his best to take care of her personal needs and those of the children. During all this time he never received any indication from his wife that she was willing to reconcile.

To the contrary, the other day his wife told him that she wants to marry another man. Evidently she had been emotionally involved with this man since the time when her husband was in the program. What blessed me in this phone call was that, after the initial shock he experienced from this news, his first concern was for her well-being.

Nevermind how it might affect him personally, he could clearly see that this wasn't God's will. She had mistakenly arrived at the conclusion that becoming involved with another man would relieve her internal misery. She was blind to the fact that she was unhappy largely because of her own selfish behavior. She had been keeping herself in a self-made prison; a prison that God has been trying to set her free from for at least three years. Her issue was no longer simply a matter of not forgiving her husband. She has been hardening her heart against God.

Eventually, after weeks of real intercession for her, he was able to confront her in a spirit of true love. Because his words obviously came from a heart of mercy, his wife was able to receive what he said. She was so touched by the spirit she sensed from him that she opened up to him like she never had before. With renewed hope, this man is now looking to God for complete reconciliation.

I don't know what the ultimate outcome will be for this particular couple, but let's for a moment consider the future for this family. What could be a better picture right now than for their kids to see daddy truly repentant for his sins and mommy truly forgiving him as Christ forgives us all? Nothing could better model to these children the love of Christ for His Church. God's love can truly be manifested through this situation if mercy is permitted to prevail. But what lesson will these children learn if mommy remarries and the family is permanently separated?

THE MERCY TEST

Perhaps nothing will reveal the reality of true Christianity like a marriage that is having difficulties. I have told my wife many times that there is absolutely no reason why a truly "Christian" marriage should ever fail, even after sexual sin has occurred.

Rose and I both had to decide that we were going to do our utmost to be Christlike in our marriage. We had to make up our minds to follow Christ in the way that He prescribes in His Word. We were either going to obey His Word or not. Most of my early "Christian" life was a farce because the commandments and requirements of Scripture had no real place in my life. Was I really a Christian? Looking back, all I can see is the life of a hypocrite: someone who talks the talk but doesn't walk the walk.

When I come across a couple who complains because Jesus expects them to show mercy toward each other, I can't help but question the reality of their commitment to Christ. I really am concerned for a lot of the people I have come in contact with over the years. It astonishes me how so many professing Christians don't live their lives according to God's Word. Their faith is something they put on at church, but the rest of their lives lack the proof that it is real. The Apostle Paul admonishes us to examine our faith. (II Corinthians 13:5) Marriage difficulties will surely test whether or not our faith is the real thing. It's when we face the tough choices that we find out if we truly do know and trust and love God.

The Word of God is clear on this matter. "He who has My commandments and keeps them, it is he who loves Me." (John 14:21a) "He who says, 'I know Him,' and does not keep His commandments, is a liar, and the truth is not in him. But whoever keeps His word, truly the love of God is perfected in him. By this we know that we are in Him. He who says he abides in Him ought himself also to walk just as He walked." (I John 2:4-6) That is what it means to be a "Christian." That word in the Greek is *Christianos*, which simply means "follower of Christ;" i.e., one who patterns his life after that of Jesus Christ.

Just growing up in church and "accepting Christ as Savior" doesn't mean that someone has truly been converted. Just saying a prayer at an altar and accepting the benefits of Christianity doesn't mean a person has become a true *follower of Christ*. A true conversion happens when a sinner is gripped with the reality that he is guilty before a Holy God. He comes to Calvary with nothing but a broken heart and a desire to be forgiven and cleansed. Through repentance and believing in what Jesus did on the Cross, he commits to live his life for Jesus. He loves God because He first loved him, and his faith is evidenced by the desire to please Him in all things.

To paraphrase Martyn Lloyd-Jones: These Beatitudes really do provide a searching test and tell us everything about our Christian profession. He continues:

> The Christian faith is not something on the surface of a man's life, it is not merely a kind of coating or veneer. No, it is something that has been happening in the very centre of his personality. That is why the New Testament talks about rebirth and being born again, about a new creation and about receiving a new nature. It is something that happens to a man at the very centre of his being; it controls all his thoughts, all his outlook, all his imagination, and, as a result, all his actions as well. All of our activities, therefore, are the result of this new nature, this new disposition which we have received from God through the Holy Spirit.[2]

If we accept this as truth, then it proves my theory that when both spouses are committed followers of Christ the odds of marital success are 100 percent! *There is absolutely no reason why a truly "Christian" marriage should ever fail, even after sexual sin has occurred.* When Christ is ruling in both hearts all things are possible. God's mercy has no limits or boundaries. Only we can limit it, by our own choices.

THE MEASURE YOU USE

When mercy is absent in a marriage it is often because one or both spouses are standing on their own righteousness. Such people hate it when God shows unadulterated mercy to a person who has sinned; especially if they feel the person hasn't earned it. At the very least they want the offender to jump through the hoops they deem necessary to earn that mercy.

If we will not learn that one thing, "I desire mercy, not sacrifice," our home will be a place of constant bickering and strife. That kind of an atmosphere is heavy with condemnation and the demand for perfection. It is an environment that is very difficult to live in. By contrast, the mercy atmosphere is light. No fight, no disagreement, no wrong done to the other, has any hope of surviving very long. Love and mutual support flourish in an atmosphere of mercy.

Doing mercy to your spouse is very simple: treat your spouse the way God has treated you. Jesus taught us:

> Be merciful, just as your Father also is merciful. Judge not, and you shall not be judged. Condemn not, and you shall not be condemned. Forgive, and you will be forgiven. Give, and it will be given to you: good measure, pressed down, shaken together, and running over will be put into your bosom. *For with the same measure that you use, it will be measured back to you.* (Luke 6:36-38 emphasis added)

This whole passage is speaking about mercy. "Give, and it will be given to you." What is it that is given? Mercy. What is it that is given in good measure, pressed down, shaken together, and running over? Mercy. What is it that is put into your bosom? A mercy heart. What is that is measured back to you in the same measure you use it? Mercy. This passage is just an elaboration of the beatitude: "Blessed are the merciful, for they will obtain mercy." (Matthew 5:7)

Cultivating an atmosphere of mercy is the only way to restore the feeling of love in your marriage. *Agape* love is a choice, and you can and must always choose to love your spouse. But if you want the feelings of love to return—that joy of being *in love* restored—you need to do mercy. You need to wash one another's feet. You need to reverse the flow of being a recipient or taker, and be a giver instead. Mercy needs to flow freely through you. When God's mercy permeates the atmosphere of your home, the qualities of love won't be lacking.

One of the greatest needs in your marriage will be free-flowing mercy toward one another. I can't tell you how many times Rose and I have needed mercy from one another. Don't be stingy with God's mercy; let it blossom and become the atmosphere of your home.

BILL AND TERI

*L*ove at first sight. There is simply no other way to describe Bill's feelings the first time he laid eyes on Teri. It happened in August, 1998 on his first day of college. Teri was a resident assistant who simply directed Bill to the right dorm. But from that day forth he only had eyes for her.

Well, that's actually only partially true. Teri was the only girl whom he was attracted to as a possible spouse. The other side of the story is that he was full of sexual lust for every girl who came across his path. Bill had been addicted to pornography for years by the time he went to college. In fact, sexual thoughts were never far from his mind.

Teri, on the other hand, grew up in a Christian family and had no aspiration other than to live a "good" life. "I would live a good life, get a good education, marry a good man, go to a good church and have a good family of my own," she remembers. "I focused on my goodness and maintaining my good standing with the Lord."

Bill took advantage of every opportunity to be around Teri. Over time, his efforts paid off and the two were soon dating on a regular basis. But from the beginning he was dishonest with her. He didn't tell her about his pornography habit or his sexual escapades. But more than that, Bill purposely set out to act like the man he thought she wanted. It didn't take him long to discover that her faith was very important to her. So, Bill learned to play the part of the Christian.

The young couple continued dating through college and married in July of 2001, just over a year after graduating college. "I remember the excitement of starting our new life together," Teri says. "We had great dreams of successful careers, children and happy living. The Lord was important but not most important. Our Christian life didn't extend much past going to church."

During the next four years, they lived the all-American life. It was, in reality, a pipe dream. As a nominal Christian, Teri lacked the discernment to realize that something was not right with Bill. The truth was that he had a thriving addiction to pornography.

One Friday Bill took off with some friends for a "boys' weekend." It was ostensibly an opportunity for the guys to get off together for some good, clean fun. Actually, they were out drinking and spending time in a strip club. That Saturday, Teri picked up Stormie Omartian's book entitled, *The Power of a Praying Wife*. When Bill returned home and saw the book sitting on the coffee table, something in him snapped. "Why do you have this?" he demanded. "Our marriage is great! Why do you feel like you have to pray for me?" The whole thing reeked of self-righteousness to him. His outburst should have alerted Teri that something was terribly wrong with him, but she simply agreed to quit reading the book.

It was about this time that their daughter was born. Instead of causing them to draw closer together, they seemed to drift further apart. It was mostly Bill who became increasingly more disconnected from Teri. When she would confront him about his aloofness, he would deny that anything was wrong. His denials were convincing and caused her to question herself, even wondering if she was imagining it all. Yet, the sense that something was wrong continued to intensify.

One day Bill failed to cover his tracks and Teri discovered a pornography site on the history of his computer. "She was heart-broken and sobbing," he recalls. "She asked me if I had been looking at pornography. At that moment, I had a choice; I could either confess or lie. I lied, lied again and lied some more."

Not long after this incident, Bill became involved in a three-month affair with a girl at work. He was wracked with guilt over his actions during the whole time. "I remember lying in bed only inches from my wife and feeling the pressing weight of guilt on my heart." Nevertheless, he refused to tell her the truth about his secret life.

On June 1, 2006, Teri confronted Bill with a cell phone bill that confirmed her suspicions that he was having an affair. "Standing in his office," she says, "my world began spinning with disbelief, shock and despair. After all, I was a good girl, married to a good guy, living a good life. This was not part of the plan!"

In the following heart-wrenching days, Teri found herself crying out to the Lord in a way she never had before. And the Lord began speaking—or, at least, she began hearing Him. "My feet hit the hot pavement one after another searching for answers, for comfort. Why God? Why? I continued walking, searching for answers. Turning the corner, God spoke—not in a loud boom—but in a clear, deep voice to my innermost heart. 'Teri, all of this has been for Satan's glory, but from now on it will all be for My glory.' This brought huge comfort to my breaking heart."

Bill confessed everything to his family and also to her parents. "During this 24-hour period—the Day of Death I've called it—filled with shock, anger, tears, yelling, screaming and flat out silence, Teri's dad asked me if I was willing to do what it took to fix the problem. 'Anything; to hell and back if need be,' was my reply."

"The double punches of adultery and pornography were hard to deal with for everyone," Teri recalls. "There were so many crushing lies, deceitfulness, betrayal... my anger was intense. By God's amazing plan, my mom knew about a place for men struggling with sexual sin—Pure Life Ministries."

On June 16, 2006, the day after their daughter's first birthday, Bill entered the Live-In program. He had had a breakthrough and had been honest for the first time in his life, but he was far from being where he needed to be spiritually. "Though I was going through this turmoil, I continued to plot and scheme, trying to make it appear that I was changing. I was trying everything I knew to get back into her good graces. One minute I was concerned about my family and the next I was plotting ways to get pornography. I was a mess!"

Bill quickly learned that his old manipulative behavior wouldn't work at PLM. "I tried to play the same religious game with Brad Furges, my counselor, that I had used with Teri. He saw right through it." It was then that Bill realized he needed to quit playing the game. He began telling his counselor things he had never told anyone before. Brad insisted that he tell Teri the whole truth—not just the edited version he had given her before. One major part of the story he had not admitted was that he had contacted his girlfriend again during the disclosure process. In spite of the possible consequences, Bill knew he had to confess it.

"After that painful phone call, I realized I had lost it all," Bill says. "Teri was just starting to believe the half-truths I was telling her and now I hit her with this. Any progress we had made was destroyed. Her response was to open a separate checking account. I had nothing left in life. It was at this point that I gave up doing things my way and really started to cry out to God for help."

"After about a month at PLM, Bill called with more devastating news," Teri remembers. "He had contacted the other girl again. This was the straw that broke the camel's back. I felt lost, not knowing what to do. How could I ever trust him again? How could I ever forgive? I remember my dad urging me to hold on. He said the PLM counselors knew what they were doing; give it more time. That night I pleaded with God for help. The next day I knew that I needed to go through the Overcomers-At-Home program."

It was after this phone call that Bill began to get serious with God. "I realized that I could never talk my way out of the mess I had made. For the first time in my life I started seeing what a sham my Christian faith had been. One day I had a gut-wrenching revelation that I was a child of darkness and desperately needed Jesus. This was a scary thing, but it was really my only option. I had nowhere left to turn but to God."

Teri was having her own revelation. "I remember getting the Bible study, *The Walk of Repentance*, and wondering why I needed to go through it. Bill was the one who needed to repent. Over the months, however, God opened my eyes to a new perspective of Him. My whole thought pattern of being a good person was shattered. God used my counselor, the books and the tapes to show me my desperate need for Jesus. Until then, I believed I was good enough. My myth of self-righteousness unraveled as I learned about my sinful nature. This was no longer just about Bill. The Bible taught me that my sins of anger, hatred, gossip, and worry were just as bad as his sin of adultery and lust. It was a truth I didn't want to acknowledge. However, there was no denying God's Word written in black and white."

In the meantime, Bill had given up on trying to convince Teri to stay with him. He had to put her in the Lord's hands and focus on getting his own life together. "I didn't write the sweet poems I once did to win her back; I didn't use sweet words to woo her back; for the first-time since I met Teri, I was relying on Jesus."

Seven months after leaving for Pure Life, Bill graduated the program and returned home. "I would be lying if I said that married life has been perfect since coming home," Bill asserts. "I can honestly say that our marriage has been real, though. There is no darkness in our marriage – no hidden sins. We have become deeply intimate with each other—bearing our souls in a way we never had in the past. Teri and I pray together, read the Bible together and grow together. I'm so thankful to Jesus for pulling me out of that darkness and revealing Himself to me. He sought me way before I started crying out to Him. Without Him I am nothing and have nothing. God is so good."

"I can remember several conversations when we both complained about this difficult change process God was putting us through," Teri adds. "I can say with certainty that I never want to go through this kind of heartbreak again, but I also wouldn't change a thing. In a way that only the Lord can do, He took a terrible situation and made it into a magnificent transformation for our marriage. We are still two sinners in daily desperate need of Jesus. We still get selfish and off-focus. We still must repent daily to the Lord and each other. But, praise God, we are living the second chance with Jesus as our focus."

*"What if God didn't design marriage
to be 'easier'? What if God had an end
in mind that went beyond our happiness,
our comfort, and our desire to be infatuated
and happy as if the world were a perfect place?
What if God designed marriage to make us
holy more than to make us happy?"*[1]

~ Gary Thomas

Chapter Seven

PURIFIED HEARTS

"Blessed are the pure in heart, for they shall see God."
(Matthew 5:8)

The marriage of Jim and Shirley represents one of those combinations that rarely occurs, when two extremely reserved and private individuals find themselves thrown together in marriage. Shirley surprised even herself when she began dating Jim at age 33; having long since assumed that she would spend the rest of her life as a single woman. Nevertheless, driven more by their hidden fear of loneliness, the unlikely pair was married in September, 1997.

It didn't take Shirley long to realize that Jim had very little love to offer her. "I felt like he still wanted to live his life as if he was single. He wanted to be his own person, and do his own thing and set his own schedule. He did not want anyone, *especially me*, interfering with his life or telling him what to do."

Jim would often go into periods of withdrawal, not saying a word, and just barely responding to any attempt Shirley would make at having a conversation with him. But perhaps the problem that puzzled her more than anything was the absence of romance and physical affection in their relationship. "I wanted his love and affection so badly, but it seemed like the more I asked for it, the more he refused. As much as I tried, I just couldn't understand what was happening, and it hurt so much that I would often cry all night long because I felt so unwanted. I felt like I was so unattractive that even my husband didn't want me."

"Shirley and I didn't fight with words; we fought with silence," Jim recalls. "I was so closed off from everyone that no one really knew me. Behind a mask of congeniality, I harbored deep shame and homosexual desires. Outwardly I was an intelligent, successful hard worker—in both my job and my religion. But nobody—absolutely nobody—was going to get a glimpse of the secrets of my heart. Even I didn't peer inside too closely."

"When conflicts arose between Jim and me, we would both tend to put up walls and 'retreat to our own corner,'" Shirley adds. "Rather than openly discussing the issue, we would live in silence, sometimes for days, making superficial conversation when necessary, but never willing to be honest about what was going on inside us."

Inevitably, the truth came out that Jim had been involved in a homosexual relationship. He eventually entered the Pure Life Ministries Live-In program and found the freedom he needed. But when Jim returned home, the two found that their communication with each other remained awkward and difficult at times.

"In the process of rebuilding our marriage I learned to be more open with Shirley," Jim states. "It was extremely uncomfortable at first. Even though I knew she loved me, she was entering into my most private thoughts and deep into my inner world. I didn't like what was in me, so it was doubly hard to let someone else see it. But we took it slowly and patiently. Things didn't change dramatically; it was a step at a time."

Over time, trust was rebuilt for both Jim and Shirley. They have learned to share their innermost thoughts and feelings and struggles with each other. Since they are both quiet by nature, they found that they had to make a conscious effort to do this. Nevertheless, they have managed to overcome the challenges involved and have found the new intimacy of their communication very rewarding.

Jim's honesty with Shirley about his struggles greatly increased her sense of security with him. Her trust for him grew as she began to see him making himself truly vulnerable with her. This was something she never saw before he went to PLM.

"One benefit to my honesty is that now I have a partner who stands with me—even when I have struggles," Jim says. "I am no longer alone in the fight. I know my wife is praying for me. Not only are the battles easier, but I have been able to experience true love and appreciation for my wife."

One of the common fallacies about marital problems is that they are the product of circumstances. Rose and I were no different. The way we saw it, my sexual sin was the foundational problem in our marriage. Of course, we assumed that once I overcame my addiction our marriage problems would be resolved. Well, the sexual sin did go, but the strife in the home still continued. We got into arguments; there were times we actually hated each other; we had trust issues, intimacy issues and times when the sun went down on our wrath. It was very difficult when we got back together after I completed the PLM Live-In program. We desperately needed to know the proper way to deal with our problems, if we were going to make it.

Many couples make the same mistake we made, which is attempting to deal with problems on a surface level. Rose and I could have easily blamed everything on my sexual sin, the pressures of ministry, our financial poverty, or any number of other things we were facing. The realization God brought to us through these different situations, however, was that we desperately needed something to change *within us*. The problem was not our outward circumstances; it was in our hearts. And we *both* needed a major internal change, not just one of us.

You see, God is seldom as concerned about fixing our

circumstances as He is in fixing "us" through them. If all we do is focus on the outward, we are in danger of missing what is vitally important to Jesus. The Pharisees missed this very thing. They were clean on the outside, yet their hearts were defiled. It was this internal corruption that made them blind, and left them unable to see God. When Jesus dealt with individuals, He always made the issues of the heart of supreme importance; and so must we if we are to see God, for it is only the pure in heart who reap the blessing of seeing God.

When Jesus said, "Blessed are the pure in heart...," He was saying, in essence, "You will be blessed as you allow the Holy Spirit to purge the sinful poison out of your heart; as that occurs, you will come into a new revelation of God." That word *pure* in the Greek is *katharos*, which means "clean (literally or figuratively), free from corrupt desire, from sin and guilt; sincere."[2]

What's more, having the heart purified means allowing God to take His rightful place within it. Rex Andrews explains the dynamics involved in this:

> A Pure Heart is a place for God...an open way from His heavenly throne to, and into, our earthly dwelling, as the extension also of His throne. But by nature the throne-place, our heart, is quite fully occupied with self. And self does not want God to rule as king... That situation shuts us out of the knowledge of [God]. To change the situation, then, requires the Heart to be purified. Only God knows how to do that.[3]

So, as we can see, the problem is within—not without. Problems cannot be effectively dealt with by focusing on outward circumstances; they can only be overcome by dealing with the heart. Those who see themselves as victims of circumstances are failing to see the greater issue involved. Such thinking, says Martyn Lloyd-Jones, "is a tragic fallacy. It overlooks the fact that it was in Paradise that man fell. It was in a perfect environment that he first went wrong, so to put man in a perfect environment cannot solve his problems."[4] Those who fantasize about having a fairytale marriage typically have the idea that if their spouse would just get it together then all their problems would be resolved.

I have had husbands and wives describe this mindset to me in different ways over the years. In one way or another, most people I meet in counseling have bought into the world's view that they are controlled by their circumstances, their feelings or by other people. They'll look anywhere to find the source of their problems except at their own selfish desires. Consequently, they've tried looking everywhere else for solutions except where God is pointing them.

Beloved, it's not about your circumstances, or your spouse; it's about God wanting to use those things to show you *your* need for a purified heart. Unless both spouses allow the Holy Spirit to deal with their natures, the problems they are facing will never be dealt with properly. God focuses on the inward because He understands that is where the problem lies. This was the gist of David's prayer when he wrote, "Search me, O God, and know my heart; try me, and know my anxieties; and see if there is any wicked way in me, and lead me in the way everlasting." (Psalm 139:23-24)

In his epistle, James pinpointed the source of marital problems when he wrote, "What causes fights and quarrels among you? Don't they come from your desires that battle within you?" (James 4:1 NIV) James exposes the very core of the real issue behind all the strife, bickering and contentions we deal with in our marriages: it is simply self-seeking and impure motives. When people are focused more on personal happiness than on pleasing God, on comfort rather than godly sacrifice, on their own ambitions rather than His eternal plan, they are acting as those who live for the things of the earth.

I know in my own life, God uses everything I encounter to show me my need for a purified heart. Just the other day, I had a run-in with a family member. This person has a very difficult nature, and I have found that I have not spiritually matured to the point where God's love always flows out of me toward this individual. In this particular situation, with minimal provocation on my part, the other person became very ugly with me. Throughout the rest of the day I kept dwelling on the hurtful things expressed to me. I became increasingly upset inside. I finally complained to the Lord, "Why is it that I am always the one who has to humble myself over and over again? They never apologize for their actions!" The more I thought of the situation, the angrier I got. Finally, the emotional pressure building up in me squeezed the words out of my heart, and I cried out: "I CANT LOVE THEM!! I'M TIRED OF THIS!! I DON'T NEED THIS ANYMORE!!"

Well, all I can say is, "Out of the abundance of the heart the mouth speaks." (Matthew 12:34) Even as the words were coming out of my mouth I knew I was wrong. Once I calmed down, I said to the Lord, *"Jesus I repent; I'm just wrong. I don't have what it takes to love as You love. Please forgive me for my unmerciful heart toward this person. Please give me Your heart and help me to love as You love. I believe You can change me and make me like You."* Once I get my heart right with the Lord, I do what I have been taught to do: I ask God to give the other person the mercies they need in life. I ask Him to meet their needs as He sees them. After praying like this the other day, the anger and resentfulness I was experiencing began to dissipate, and within a short time God was able to change my heart toward that person.

The tendency to protect myself is so ingrained in my nature that I will probably have to learn this lesson many times before I get total victory in this area of my life. Yet, each time I repent over one of these failures, I can tell that the Lord is gaining ground in my heart.

This particular incident didn't occur within the confines of a marital relationship but the dynamics are still the same. If we will allow Him to, the Lord will use our marital problems to show us how greatly we need our hearts to be purified.

BEING VULNERABLE: TRUTH IN THE INWARD PARTS

As Rose and I started learning to do the words of Jesus toward one another in a practical way, we found our marriage progressing down the pathway of God's healing, cleansing and restoration. He did things that we never thought would be possible given the years of sin, mistrust and defilement that had occurred. Nonetheless, we were both dealing with a lot of issues and baggage, all of which served to magnify our need for a pure heart.

One of the major issues we faced was rebuilding trust. Naturally, Rose's trust for me was destroyed by my years of deception and selfishness. Over and over again I had proved to her that I was only concerned about myself and that, when it came right down to it, I would lie to cover up my actions. She had learned to be guarded with me. The way I treated her had caused her to erect protective walls around her heart. She constantly lived with the fear that I would fall back into my sin.

My first reaction to her obvious distrust of me was to try to convince her that I was now trustworthy. When she still resisted my best attempts to win her over, I would get angry with her. This only reinforced her concerns that I had not changed.

Rose came to trust me over time, but it didn't happen the way I expected. It came about as I started opening up to her and being honest about my struggles. In the past, I lived for myself and didn't include Rose in the innermost part of my life. I was neither truthful nor vulnerable with my wife. I want to say to all of the husbands reading this; your wives want to know you—all of you, everything about you, your deepest thoughts, your innermost feelings, your fears; yes, even your struggles. Undoubtedly, that sounds very frightening to a man who has been immersed in the duplicity of sexual sin. But I have heard from my own wife, as well as many of the wives she has counseled, that the dishonesty was worse to them than the actual sexual sin. Such deception cuts a wife deeply; consequently distrust is one of the main issues nearly every couple must overcome after sexual sin has occurred.

Obviously, it was primarily my responsibility to change the situation. That meant I had to change the way I interacted with Rose. I had to starting being honest with her in spite of how she might react. If you think about it, when we lie we are only thinking about protecting ourselves. It's the total opposite of putting the other person's interests before our own.

As a counselor, I have encountered many husbands who still hadn't told their wives the full truth about the extent of their sin, insisting that they didn't want to hurt their wives any further by telling them. They forget they are talking to a former con. The truth of the matter is that these men just don't want to have to deal with the aftermath. And worse yet, they're still resisting the vulnerability that is going to be necessary if their marriage is going to make it. Truth and ongoing vulnerability insulate a marriage from the deception of adultery, while secrets keep the door ajar for a future plunge back into adultery.

I know for myself, when I was finally exposed and told my wife everything, it was like an enormous weight lifted off my shoulders. Being utterly honest with my wife was only the beginning, though. I also needed to really make myself vulnerable to her. It meant sharing everything going on inside even when she didn't ask. Rose had given her heart to me fully when we got married. She made herself totally vulnerable to me. To this day, I grieve over the way I trounced on her deepest being.

BEING REALLY VULNERABLE: THE MARRIAGE BED

Rebuilding trust in our marriage was one major area affected by our pursuit of a pure heart. The second area was our marriage bed, which had been defiled and rendered impure by my sexual sin. This is most certainly a critical issue for couples dealing with the aftermath of sexual sin, but it is also an issue for many others who, simply because of their past experiences or failures, have brought baggage into their sexual relationship.

Quite often, couples have been sexually involved before their wedding day. Even if they repent and then abstain from it, there is still the guilt of knowing they have sinned and wishing they had waited. Then when sexual sin invades the relationship, the marriage bed issues are only made all the worse. Under such conditions, sexual intimacy may understandably seem awkward, tense and guilt-ridden, perhaps for some, even dirty. Couples in these circumstances despair to even consider the possibility that they can have pure hearts before God in the marriage bed.

To anyone who feels that way, I affirm to you by the truth of God's Word and my personal testimony that God is able to make all things new. That is the hope of our salvation. That is what Jesus accomplished on the Cross. His blood is able to wash away the guilt of sin, the penalty of sin and the effects of sin.

When God created man and woman He looked at all He had done and it was pleasing in His eyes. Scripture records: "Then God saw everything that He had made, and indeed it was very good." (Genesis 1:31) The word "everything" must include the way He made and designed our bodies, does it not? I say that because the goodness of God's original creation is foundational to understanding and accepting His intention that we enjoy one another through sexual relations within the covenant of marriage. Kay Arthur explains: "God designed us in such a way that the greatest excitement the nerve endings of our bodies can ever experience happens in the process of sexual intercourse.

He *built* us that way. As the woman receives her husband into herself, they experience a oneness beyond what they will ever know with any other human being."[5] Sexual relations were designed by God for procreation, but also as a time of giving and expressing our love to one another by the giving our body to bring pleasure and delight to each other.

Rose and I realized we had to consciously put behind us all of the old and start focusing on the new. That meant putting our past failures under the blood, and beginning the process of being made new in all things. We had to learn to bring godly convictions into our lovemaking. I wanted my time with her to be a time of expressing my love to her, not a time to satisfy lust. God was doing a work in my heart and I wanted it to show in the marriage bed.

Having the mind of Christ means putting others' interests before your own, which is precisely what I needed to learn to do with Rose. I learned to ask questions about our lovemaking, what pleased her, what made her uncomfortable, and what I could do to help her with any of the issues she might be dealing with. Open communication is vital in learning to look out for the interest of your mate in bed. In addition, Rose and I would often pray together, asking God to bless our time together and for Him to be in our midst.

Rose had to learn not to be focused on what I was thinking. Wives tend to wonder things like, "Did he do this with so and so?" "Is he fantasizing about a past experience?" "Is he comparing me with someone else?" Rose had to choose to get her focus off herself and off of what I was thinking, and focus on giving herself to be a blessing during our time together.

I know for myself, I have found that putting my wife's needs before my own truly is the way of blessing. When God is in the midst of our lovemaking, and we are focusing on pleasing Him and our spouse, there is a oneness involved that is beautiful, fulfilling and lasting, (unlike lust which is fleeting, unfulfilling and ugly). There is a bond made between the husband and the wife that only God can bring about. It expresses and glorifies God's love when we can share ourselves in this way together.

We would do well to remember, however, that this all starts long before we get into the bedroom. If we aren't practicing unselfishness toward each other during the day, we won't do it in the bedroom. The time a couple spends in sexual intimacy should be a natural extension of what is already taking place on a daily basis within their relationship. The marriage bed is made pure when the heart of each spouse is made pure.

In fact, a pure heart renders all things pure. "If the heart is pure," said Charles Finney, "the life not only ought to be pure but will be. If the heart of a man be pure, all else will be pure—all his activities—all he does as well as all he says. If any of us suppose that our hearts are better than our lives, we are fundamentally deceived. Nothing can be pure if the heart is not; and nothing can be impure if the heart be really pure."[6] Allow God to purify your hearts. As you do, you will find a pure marriage emerging out of the ash heap of past failure.

*"If God be our Father, we are of
peaceable spirits—'Blessed be the peacemakers,
they shall be called the children of God.' Grace infuseth
a sweet, amicable disposition; it files off the ruggedness of men's
spirits; it turns the lion-like fierceness into a lamb-like
gentleness. They, who have God to be their Father,
follow peace as well as holiness."*[1]

Chapter Eight

A PLACE OF PEACE

"Blessed are the peacemakers, for they shall be called sons of God."
(Matthew 5:9)

Ken and Julie met each other at a party. They quickly discovered they had a lot in common, and before long decided to get married. In spite of their partying lifestyle, they got along remarkably well. For the first time in Julie's life, she felt truly loved by a man. And Ken had finally found someone who appreciated him. The couple found much comfort in each other.

Eventually they both got saved. However, the closeness they had enjoyed as a couple inexplicably began to evaporate. In fact, the more they both pursued the things of God, the more they argued and bickered! "I could not figure out why," Julie shares. "I started to not even want to be around him, especially if he wanted to talk about the Lord or read something in the Bible. It annoyed me so much."

"We couldn't stand each other," Ken agrees. "We could only get along at church and around our church friends, but at home it was pure 'weeping and gnashing of teeth.'" To keep the illusion of peace, the couple began avoiding each other altogether.

Their marriage was in trouble and neither one of them knew what to do to straighten it out. It was then that Julie's brother convinced them to attend the Pure Life Ministries annual conference with him. They were so affected by the presence of God in those meetings that they immediately entered the Overcomers At-Home Program.

During counseling, Julie came to realize that her controlling nature was causing a lot of the problems the couple was experiencing. When her husband had simply been a drug addict, he wasn't concerned about any of this. Being high had masked many of the latent problems at work in their marriage.

Ken began to see how he had been trying to fix their problems through his own strength. Over time he came to learn how to turn to the Lord in the midst of conflict.

Issues still come up occasionally for Ken and Julie. But a noticeable sense of peace has pervaded their home. Both spouses are regularly praying for each other. Conflicts are resolved through mature discussion. And more than anything, they have both been deeply impacted by the Prince of Peace!

The crowning glory of a life that has been truly conquered by the Holy Spirit is peace: peace with God and peace with others. The basic meaning of the word peace, whether it be in Hebrew (*shalom*), Greek (*eirene*) or English, is the quiet atmosphere that comes when there is no strife. A peacemaker then, is someone who is able to reconcile individuals who have been at variance with each other. As we will soon see, this becomes a prominent feature of a godly marriage.

Undoubtedly, everyone longs for peace: when all the waves of doubt and fear are stilled, when anxious thoughts are silenced, when disturbed and enflamed emotions are calmed and when all inner conflicts cease. Who wouldn't want to enjoy such a tranquil life? But it is not enough to be a mere peace-lover; we are called to be peacemakers.

However, our peacemaking efforts will only be successful if we first understand that there are two types of peace. There is the peace that the world gives, and there is the peace of God.

The former type of peace is false. It is superficial and essentially meaningless. It is what the world offers. But we must remember that this world is ruled by a rebel prince and is in rebellion to God's authority. Consequently, it is normal to be in a state of "peace" for the person who is walking "according to the course of this world, according to the prince of the power of the air, the spirit who now works in the sons of disobedience." (Ephesians 2:2b) Truth be told, however, if a person does not feel himself to be in a very real war with the world around him something is terribly wrong with his spiritual life. The peace that the world gives is nothing but an alliance the devil makes with a person's flesh.

Even people who profess to be followers of Christ can be in a false peace. They are happy and content to live for the pleasures and comforts of the world. But as soon as the Holy Spirit begins to put His finger on some pet idol or favorite sin, suddenly their peace is gone. The truth of the matter is that the peace they seem to possess is actually an indication of how hardhearted they have become. Their conscience can no longer detect the conviction of the Holy Spirit.

This is the peace that the world offers. It is the feigned friendship of an enemy who smiles to your face but harbors hatred for you in his heart.

This explains the seeming contradiction we encounter when the "Prince of Peace" exclaimed, "Do not think that I came to bring peace on earth. I did not come to bring peace but a sword." (Mark 10:34) It is not possible for true followers of Jesus Christ to be at peace with the devil's system.

Yet, there is another kind of peace: "My peace I give to you; not as the world gives do I give to you." Jesus says. (John 14:27) "In Me you may have peace. In the world you will have tribulation; but be of good cheer, I have overcome the world." (John 16:33) Jesus offers peace to anyone who is willing to repent of his rebellion to God's authority. What Jesus did for us on the Cross at the expense of His own life is proof that God seeks to reconcile us with Himself. When a person is in right relationship with God he comes into union with Him. When you are one with this Being of love the essence of His nature will flow out of you.

These two types of peace are also evident in the different perspectives found in God's kingdom and the Kingdom of Darkness. These conflicting points of view are brought out in James 3:

> Who is wise and understanding among you? Let him show by good conduct that his works are done in the meekness of wisdom.
>
> But if you have bitter envy and self-seeking in your hearts, do not boast and lie against the truth. This wisdom does not descend from above, but is earthly, sensual, demonic. For where envy and self-seeking exist, confusion and every evil thing are there.
>
> But the wisdom that is from above is first pure, then peaceable, gentle, willing to yield, full of mercy and good fruits, without partiality and without hypocrisy. Now the fruit of righteousness is sown in peace by those who make peace. (James 3:13-18)

Consider the world's mentality. Everything Satan offers people caters to the lusts of their flesh. The reason there is so much strife in this world is that there are roughly six billion people going after what their flesh desires. It only stands to reason that people will be competing for the same carnal prizes. There is only so much to go around. Yes, it is true, that there is a certain kind of peace in the midst of all of this chaos because everyone holds the same basic values.

But James says that this kind of wisdom is "earthly, sensual, demonic." Why is that? "For where envy and self-seeking exist, confusion and every evil thing are there." The world's wisdom (which is often repackaged and promoted through Christian bookstores) is an alternative to the Cross—the place where people lay down their selfish ambitions and give their wills to God.

By contrast, God's wisdom has a completely different fragrance. One doesn't sense the odor of Self in it. People operating in this mindset tend to value the lives of others. Their driving ambition in life is not to push others out of the way so that they might achieve some prize. What they consider to be a prize is the welfare of others. Instead of living for Self, they live for Christ.

All of these qualities can be summed up in one word: LOVE. Love is a choice to deny our selfish and carnal way of thinking, choosing instead to conform our minds and our deeds to God's way of thinking. Love always revolves around the needs of others at the sacrifice of my own desires. Those who are willing to surrender to God in this way find the promised blessing of a harvest of righteousness in their home—harmony between individuals, a prevailing calmness, and a peaceful mind that is free from fears, agitating passions and moral conflicts.

A person with that kind of mindset is always going to bring about a peaceful atmosphere. Martyn Lloyd Jones writes:

> The explanation of all of our troubles is human lust, greed, selfishness, self-centeredness, it is the cause of all the trouble and discord, whether between individuals, or between groups within a nation, or between nations themselves. Before one can be made a peacemaker one must be entirely delivered from self, from self interest, from self concern. Before you can be a peacemaker you really must be entirely forgetful of self because as long as you are thinking about yourself, you cannot be doing the work properly. To be a peacemaker you must be as it were, absolutely neutral so that you can bring the two sides together.

PEACE IN THE HOME

Marriage is said to be the consummation of two people's lives. When Christ is allowed to be in the center of that relationship, the two become one.

Thus, the last beatitude is the culmination of the previous six. As Rose and I have allowed the Holy Spirit to do His work in our hearts, a noticeable atmosphere of peace has prevailed in our home. There was a time that our home was full of variance, discord and strife. But today it truly is a place of peace. (Of course that's not to say that at times the seas don't kick up a bit!)

There are a number of things I would like to touch on here that will promote this kind of atmosphere in the home.

The first thing I need to say is that you will never find peace in the world. It is an interesting phenomenon that Christians with inner turmoil often turn to the world—a place of darkness and chaos—for peace. Rather than go to the One who offers true inner peace, they turn to television or some other form of entertainment to be temporarily distracted (sedated) from their sense of turmoil. Predictably, as soon as the program is over or they finish reading the article, the lack of peace is there awaiting them. Too many times Christians give God a portion of their hearts but hold onto the things of this world that they love.

It should go without saying by this point in the book that it is only in Jesus Christ that believers will ever experience joy, peace and fulfillment. Paul wrote, "For those who live according to the flesh set their minds on the things of the flesh, but those who live according to the Spirit, the things of the Spirit. For to be carnally minded is death, but to be spiritually minded is life and peace." (Romans 8:5-6) When a Christian is truly walking in the Spirit, there will be a sense of peacefulness that will prevail in his life.

As we have already discussed, the world has no true peace to offer a believer. In fact, the more a Christian spends time in the world's atmosphere, the less peace he or she will experience in life. Television programs that agitate the flesh may be temporarily exciting, but they also rob a person of the peace which God offers. In Philippians 4, Paul tells his readers that if they will "meditate on" godly things, "the God of peace will be with you." (Philippians 4:9)

Another thing that promotes peace within the home is loving communication. Words are powerful and will either work to bring about God's peace and unity in a marriage, or they will work to bring about contention, strife and division. The way a Christian talks to others is often a gauge to what is going on inside. Jesus said, "out of the abundance of the heart the mouth speaks." (Matthew 12:34)

There have been times when I have counseled "Christian" couples and watched them shred each other to pieces with their words. Words can be very damaging to the unity and peace of a relationship. God intends for our words to edify one another, to build up and to bring grace to each other.

Fostering peace in the home also depends a great deal upon the way in which a couple handles the differences that are sure to come up in life. It is so important for a Christian couple to be able to maturely and biblically address issues that arise.

A "conference table" is a good way to accomplish that. This is a scheduled time a couple sets aside every week to sit down, without interruption, for the express purpose of dealing with things that have come up during that week. To do this properly, it is vital that each session begins and ends in prayer. A Bible should be on hand as the primary source of wisdom in resolving conflicts. I say "primary," not in the sense that there can be any other source, but because there are many godly books that are biblically based that can also be helpful.

The conference table is a time when each person can repent of wrong attitudes or sinful actions and seek to bring down any walls that have been erected. I know for Rose and me that whenever we sit down and do this, the first thing we have learned to do is to repent to one another for anything in our own hearts that wasn't right. After forgiving one another we can then look at the situation through God's eyes rather than our own. He has always helped us to overcome our problems when we have been willing to come together in this way.

The conference table can also be a time of correcting or disciplining a child. It can be a time of prayer and seeking God's wisdom in His word for a decision. Whatever the situation, the conference table will be a place where true godly communication takes place in your home. The husband should lead in this process and should keep things centered on God's Word.

These are a few of the things that Rose and I have instituted into our lives that have helped to establish godly harmony in our home. I am sometimes amazed at how the Lord has made us one in Him. There are times when we have ministered together that He was able to speak His heart simultaneously through both of us. Other times in prayer or in a chapel meeting one of us will say what the other was thinking. Most of all, I am amazed at how He has blessed us with His peace in our home. People who have visited our home have actually said to us that they sensed the peace there. Praise the Lord! That is what He wants, our lives and our marriage to promote His peace to those around us.

Beloved, my hope is that you are beginning to see the benefit of fighting for a marriage like this. Do not grow weary in the process. It will take some time, but God will bring forth a harvest of peace in your situation as well. He wants you to be one with Him and to know Him in all of His glory. That is the only way you can arrive at this last beatitude and experience the intended purpose that God has in mind.

When we are complete in Him, our home, and our marriage will be a place of peace, and then God will use us to bring that peace to others. By this we will be known as His children and He will be glorified.

This is a process that takes time and perseverance to accomplish. Please don't miss out on the blessed union God desires to have with you and your spouse. Don't allow your marriage difficulties to hinder Him from being glorified through your lives. God is able to bring any marriage out of the ashes and into His beauty. People need to see that He is still the God of miracles and that nothing is too difficult for Him.

CARL AND LINDA

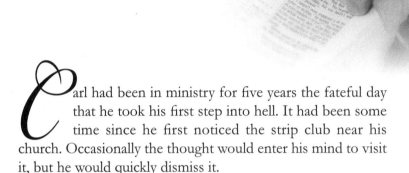

*C*arl had been in ministry for five years the fateful day that he took his first step into hell. It had been some time since he first noticed the strip club near his church. Occasionally the thought would enter his mind to visit it, but he would quickly dismiss it.

The fact that he was a happily married youth pastor didn't seem to diminish his curiosity about what was within the battered walls of that dilapidated building. He often toyed with the thought of visiting the place, and over time his resolve to resist the temptation waned.

One day, he impulsively but very purposefully pushed his nagging fears aside. With a pounding heart and shortness of breath Carl made the quick jaunt to the club. It was almost as if he was watching someone else go through the motions in his body. He could hardly believe he was actually handing his cash to the man at the front door.

The next few moments seemed to be a blur of overwhelming excitement and fear—the two passions working together to accelerate the exhilaration he was experiencing. As his eyes adjusted to the darkness, he took trembling steps toward a seat near the stage. Carl was stunned by what he saw that day...no; he was hooked.

An hour or so later he darted out of this hellish den where lust-filled men and hollowed women partner together down the long, miserable descent into ignominy. Carl, a minister of Jesus Christ, had joined their club.

"The truly amazing thing is that for the next eighteen years I was able to juggle my secret life of prostitutes, massage parlors and strip clubs with an increasingly successful ministry," Carl relates. "No one, including my wife, had a clue as to who I really was. I was a classic Pharisee. I looked so good on the outside, but inside I was full of dead man's bones."

Eventually Carl began stealing money from his church to cover the cost of his ever-burgeoning addiction. In the insanity of his thinking, he also kept detailed records of the thousands of dollars he had stolen thinking he would somehow pay it back without anyone ever finding out.

"Had I been left to myself, I would still be living in that hell. 'But God, who is rich in mercy...' intervened in my life and exposed me," continues Carl. It happened when his wife discovered a secret bank account he had opened. Within a week he was forced to fully confess his secret life to his church board. "I resigned my position as pastor—something in my delusion I had never thought would really happen."

By chance, it was just at that time that he received a brochure in the mail describing Pure Life Ministries. He checked into it further and read Steve Gallagher's story. Steve's testimony breathed hope and Carl began wondering if he could actually find freedom from his sin there.

"I was devastated when my husband confessed the extent of his sexual sin to me," remembers Linda. "I immediately decided to file for divorce—if for no other reason than to protect myself financially and emotionally. My son pleaded with me not to divorce his dad and for his sake I agreed to then get a separation. Since I was the church secretary and we lived in the church parsonage, I suddenly found myself without a job, a home, a church, a husband and a support system."

"My wife began divorce proceedings. There was also talk at the church about prosecuting me for embezzling funds. At that point it seemed certain that I was not only headed for divorce court but criminal court as well. I realized that I could very well end up in prison."

Nevertheless, Carl's main concern was getting the help he needed. He entered the Pure Life Ministries Live-In program in December, 2000. "God had me right where he wanted me to be. I was now in a place where He could break me and begin reshaping my life into the image of Jesus Christ. I had not been there long when the Lord began to deal severely with me. I was now face to face with who I really was: a deceiver, an adulterer and a thief. I had to face the fact that I was so self-centered that I had been willing to hurt anyone as long as I could have the pleasure of that one moment."

Carl was facing the greatest crisis of his life. One day, the reality of all that he had done overwhelmed him. He ended up on his face before the Lord truly repenting—not simply about the sinful things he had done but the person he had become. It was as if God was purging the love of evil out of the deepest part of his being.

From that point on his life took a completely different course. Scriptures that he had been so familiar with in the past—and had even used in sermons—were now becoming reality to him. They were no longer just words on a page. He began seeing Christ in a new dimension and discovered how deep His love was for him. His prayer time came alive for the first time in his life. He also learned the importance of living in daily repentance.

"I was now living in the light and learning how to be free from the power of sin. Through the ministry of PLM I was able to see Jesus Christ like never before. I began to better understand the depth of His love and mercy for me. I discovered how much

I needed Him in my life every day. Seeing Jesus for who He really is ignited a desire in me to become more like Him."

While Carl was having a spiritual awakening, Linda was spiraling into a deep depression. She could not understand how she could be so naïve and undiscerning that her husband could be involved in this level of sin for 18 years without her knowing it. At times she felt like she was losing her mind. Despair overwhelmed her.

But God stepped into her dark world and began to reveal Himself in a fresh, new way. He provided Linda with a good job, a nice place to live and a solid church home. "God became my everything," she says. "He was my provider, deliverer, defender, comforter, counselor and faithful friend. This was a bitter-sweet time. It was hard and difficult, yet there was a sweetness in the suffering as I drew closer to Christ. My strength grew, as I became more dependent on God. I came to realize that I didn't need a husband but I definitely did need God."

Linda made one visit to Carl during his stay at Pure Life. "I actually only went to tell him how much he had hurt me." What she didn't expect, was the complete change that had occurred in him. "I was pleasantly surprised and intrigued when I spent time with him for the first time. What impressed me the most was the meekness and humility I saw in him. He was so different than before; but I was not ready to have him back in my life. I needed to know that this was real and lasting."

Linda struggled for a long time with bitterness, self-righteousness and unforgiveness. She wanted to please God but real forgiveness seemed so unattainable to her. "God was dealing with my heart," she confesses. "I knew I needed to die to my own selfishness and pride. I learned a lot about how deep, wide, long and high the love of God is during that time. The Lord began to open my heart to see that I expected others to forgive me when I wronged them, but I was unwilling to extend that same forgiveness to Carl. Little by little my heart softened."

Carl graduated the program in August, 2001. Since his wife wasn't willing to reconcile, he decided to stay in Kentucky. His church board graciously agreed to allow him to repay the church over time. He continued working at the factory job he got while in the program, sending every extra dime he earned to his wife and to the church. It took him seven years to do it, but he repaid every cent he owed the church.

After watching the fruits of repentance in Carl's life, Linda decided to reconcile with him. Two years after their separation and one year after his graduation from Pure Life, Carl moved back in with his wife.

"God helped me stay free from my sinful past and after two years of separation my wife and I fully reconciled. Joy has entered back into our lives. We're able to talk about the future with hope and we're now able to dream again. Daily repentance will always be necessary because I want to keep growing into the image of Christ. I've been working at loving my wife more and thinking of her needs. Again, there's much room for improvement, but I'm honestly trying to grow in this area."

Linda adds, "I am grateful God has given us a second chance at marriage. We now attempt to make our relationship with God and each other a priority, knowing that is what will keep us on the right path. We hold each other accountable for finances and time spent with the Lord, and if we feel something is slipping we talk about it instead of letting it go. My hope and trust is in God and I now know I can do all things through Christ who strengthens me. God is continuing to transform us into His likeness. While my husband was at PLM he sent me a plaque with a picture of a butterfly and words that simply said, 'With God all things are possible.' We keep it displayed in our living room as a reminder of what God has done in our lives. He truly is a God of mercy, forgiveness and restoration."

"I deserved divorce, prison and eternal death for the things I had done," Carl exclaims. "It is not possible for me to fully explain the wonderful difference that Christ has made in my life. I owe Him everything. He has done the impossible! He has set me free, changed my heart and restored my life. All the honor and praise goes to Him for He is truly worthy."

EPILOGUE

TO GOD BE THE GLORY

*I*n 2006 Rose and I had the privilege to minister in Hawaii. On the last Sunday of our trip we were invited to share our testimony at a church on the west side of Kauai. I remember sitting on a stool behind my wife as she shared her side of our story and what God had brought us through. It was like someone turned on a video in my mind as I sat and re-lived all that had happened. It had been a long time since I paused to consider all we went through and how hard it was at the time. I thought to myself, *God how did we get here? What are we doing in Hawaii sharing our testimony? We shouldn't even be married.* As I contemplated the goodness of God, I began to get overwhelmed and started to weep uncontrollably. When it was my time to get up and share I could hardly get a word out. I just stood there and wept before the crowd. All I could say was, "God is so good." Over and over the same phrase kept pouring out, "God is so good."

When we concluded our testimony it was obvious to all that God had done a miracle in our marriage. It reminds me of what happened in the book of Nehemiah. After completing the seemingly impossible task of rebuilding the walls of Jerusalem,

Nehemiah gives this account of their success, "So the wall was finished on the twenty-fifth day of Elul, in fifty-two days. And it happened, when all our enemies heard of it, and all the nations around us saw these things, that they were very disheartened in their own eyes; *for they perceived that this work was done by our God.*" (Nehemiah 6:15-16, emphasis added) God was glorified! That is what God can do when we trust Him and yield to His plan for our lives and our marriage.

Our lives and our marriage are the stage upon which God desires to manifest Himself to those around us. I can't tell you how many times Rose and I have been able to give hope to others because of what God has been able to accomplish in us. Your situation is no different. When the Beatitudes described in this book become a reality in your lives, your marriage will reflect His glory and exalt His name in the eyes of an unbelieving world. And that, beloved, has been God's plan and purpose all along. To God be the Glory!

STUDY GUIDE

*P*lease take your time as you go through this Study Guide, spending at least a week on each chapter. On the practical side, you'll probably want to use a notebook or journal to record your answers and the insights gained as you go through this Study Guide. Also, each spouse should do the questions separately (except in a few instances where the question dictates otherwise). At the end of each week you can share with one another what God has been showing you. On the spiritual side, I ask that you approach each question prayerfully and with an open heart. You will only get as much out of this as you put into it.

1. "Both society and the Church suffer from a lack of understanding about relationships. But God is concerned about relationships and has given us much instruction about how to fulfill His will in relating to Him and others. Relationships are not static things; they are either getting worse or getting better. They take work!" [Stuart Scott, *The Exemplary Husband: Teacher's Guide,* Bemidji, MN: Focus Publishing, 2002, p. 15.] With this in mind:

    a) Take some time and rate your marriage (see Appendix A).

    b) Since you recited your vows, has your marriage been getting better or worse? Please explain your response.

2. Before reading the rest of the book, stop, count the cost, and if you are willing, pray a prayer of commitment to believe and obey God's Word as it is presented in the rest of the book. Also review and sign (together with your spouse, if possible) the Restoring Covenant pledge (see Appendix B).

3. Examine your heart and ask yourself, "Did I come into my marriage with a list of expectations?" If so, make a list of them.

    a) Review your list of expectations and try to determine what each one is based on. Is it Biblical truth? A selfish desire? A fantasy formed from movies or romance books? A family tradition?

    b) If the expectation is not from a Biblical truth, are you willing to surrender it to the Lord?

4. Look up the definition of the word "blessed" in the Vine's dictionary (or a comparable Bible dictionary) and write down its meaning.

5. According to the author, what will begin to happen in the marriage relationship as each spouse starts concentrating on and repenting of their own sin, rather than focusing on the faults of their mate?

6. According to the author, what will produce a fulfilling marriage?

7. Jesus said in Mark 3:25 that "if a house is divided against itself, that house cannot stand." How would this verse apply to the marital relationship?

8. How does *your* heart need to change toward your spouse if God is to be glorified in your marriage?

9. What is the intent of this book?

1. After reading this chapter, describe in your own words what it means to be "poor in spirit."

2. How has God used your present situation to bring you into the reality that *you don't have what it takes* to make your marriage work?

3. Hebrews 12:1-2 admonishes us to, "throw off everything that hinders and the sin that so easily entangles, and let us run with perseverance the race marked out for us...fixing our eyes on Jesus..."

   a) Are there things in your life that are hindering you from becoming poor in spirit? What resources, abilities and strengths in your own life need to be "thrown off?" Make a list.

   b) Are you willing to fix your eyes on Jesus and repent of and surrender these things one by one, so that God can begin the work of restoration in your marriage?

4. What did Jesus mean when He said, "...unless you are converted and become as little children..."?

5. What does the author identify as "a pernicious attitude that keeps people from seeing their need to live in daily repentance before God"?

6. Please write out the paragraph that starts with "Before a marriage can be rebuilt..."

7. Memorize this quote: "If someone offends you, ask the Lord what kind of miserable flesh is left in me that still gets offended." Use this often to help you see what God is trying to show you about yourself.

8. List the three specific things the author suggests that couples should pray as they begin rebuilding their marriage. Are you willing to commit to doing these three things?

9. In Miracle Marriage Number One, what needed to happen in Danny's life before he could really love Paula and his kids? What did Paula need to come to terms with (acknowledge) in order to get the breakthrough she needed? What necessary ingredients made the restoration of their marriage possible?

10. Pray the following prayer, or write one of your own, and begin to pray regularly for poverty of spirit.

Father,
Please make me poor in spirit.
I ask in your mercy that you would
gently bring me down out of my pride
and self-righteous attitude toward my spouse.
Help me to see my neediness. Help me to see myself
in light of You. Father, put me in my rightful place
before You so You can be glorified in my
marriage. In Jesus' name I pray.
AMEN.

1. What does the author mean when he states, "Each spouse must face the cross for themselves in this journey of restoration"?

2. Read Luke 18:9-14. In terms of seeing your own need and being broken over what you're like inside, do you most resemble the Pharisee or the Publican (Tax Collector)? Please explain your answer.

3. How do you view your spouse's sin (sinful nature)? Do you see how it will harm him/her, or are you only concerned with how it is affecting you? Please explain your answer.

4. Complete the *Log List* assignment in Appendix C.

5. What does it mean to "be nothing" from a biblical view?

6. Do your thoughts, words, and actions most resemble Saul or David when you are made aware of your own sin? Explain your answer.

7. List the 7 fruits of Godly Sorrow.

8. Read through the Sermon on the Mount (Matthew 5 -7), then complete Part A of the assignment in Appendix D. Also begin Part B of this assignment and continue it daily until you complete it.

9. The author writes, "We have all been called to be mourners and sufferers with Christ." According to the author, what is our consolation?

1. Read through the "Biblical Roles of a Husband and Wife" article in Appendix E.

    a) List the specific areas of your marriage where you are not fulfilling your role as a husband or wife.

    b) Go down your list and seek to implement a plan of action to better fulfill your role according to the Word of God.

2. According to the author, what two things "are meant to bring the Christian into a greater submission to the lordship of Jesus Christ"?

3. Write out the definition of meekness as given by Rex Andrews in the chapter.

4. According to the author, "in marriage, many times the solution to a problem is simply to say" what?

5. Read and meditate on Isaiah 53. In light of Jesus' submission to the Father, what excuse, if any, do you have to not submit to God's Word? Explain your answer.

6. Memorize II Timothy 3:16-17.

7. Pray through the four elements of II Timothy 3:16-17. Are they true in your own life regarding how the Bible affects you? Which areas do you need to change?

8. The book of Proverbs has much to say about a wise and foolish person with regard to hearing and receiving reproof and correction. Find and write out 10 of these verses from Proverbs (looking up the words *wise* or *fool* in a concordance may help you). Do you resemble a foolish person or a wise person?

9. According to the author, the Word of God must become the _____ _____ by which a couple is led and guided.

1. According to the author, "Seeking God and His righteousness must be one of the _____ _____ of life."

2. Read Psalm 63:1. Does this verse describe your hunger for God?

3. What is *kosmos*?

4. Take a survey of your "free" time for a week. How much time do you spend in prayer, in reading your Bible, in reading materials that nourish your soul? How much time do you spend on other things? (e.g., TV, movies, web surfing, emails, video games, shopping, talking on phone, exercising, and so forth). Are any of your free time activities carnal or in some way spiritually detrimental for you?

5. Take a spiritual inventory of the atmosphere in your home: is your home conducive to seeking God or is it influenced by of the spirit of the world? Discuss with your spouse magazines, music, or any other worldly influences that are in your home that might need to go. Is it time to purge your DVD collection? (Do you have movies would you not want Jesus to watch with you?)

6. Read I Corinthians 15:33 and II Corinthians 6:14. In light of Paul's warnings, do you need to reevaluate any of your friendships?

7. Are you prepared to make a move, change careers, and downsize a home in order to follow God's call on your life? What might hinder you the most?

8. Using the article "Developing a Devotional Time" found in Appendix F, prepare and implement a plan for your daily Bible reading and prayer time.

9. Suggested reading: *Intoxicated With Babylon* by Steve Gallagher.

1. How much debt has your heavenly Father forgiven for you? Do you act like the servant in Matthew 18: 23-35 when your spouse asks you to forgive his/her debt?

2. Read I Corinthians 13:1-8 and apply it to your marriage. Prayerfully review the "Love Test" in Appendix G.

3. God entreats us to ask Him for what we don't have in ourselves. Ask the Lord to transform your heart and to teach you how to love your spouse (see Appendix H).

4. Write out 20 things about your spouse you are grateful for, then frame it and give it to him/her.

5. Make a list of some ways you can show love to your spouse and focus on him/her as God's son or daughter, rather than looking out for your own interest. Try to implement at least one or two of these each week.

6. Prayerfully review the "One Another Passages" in Appendix I; allow the Lord to work these commands into your heart.

7. Memorize the definition of mercy at the beginning of this chapter. Let the truth of it convict and convince you to live God's way, freely giving mercy as you have received it yourself from Him.

8. Pray the *Prayer of Mercy* outline every day this week for your spouse (see Appendix J).

1. In this chapter, the author states: "Many couples make the same mistake we made, which is attempting to deal with problems on a surface level." Has this been an issue in your marriage? Can you now identify the heart issues involved? Write a 1-2 page commentary on this "common mistake" as it applies in your marriage, citing specific examples of the surface problems you have faced as well as the heart issues involved.

2. In Psalm 51:6 we read, "God desires truth in the inward parts." Are you willing to be honest with your spouse as to what is in your heart? List specific ways have you been unwilling to live in the light with your spouse and be prepared to share them (involve your pastor/counselor if necessary).

3. According to the author, "James exposes the very core of the real issue behind all the strife, bickering and contentions we deal with in our marriages." What is the core issue?

4. According to the author, " _____ _____ _____ _____ _____ insulate a marriage from the deception of adultery, while _____ keep the door ajar for a future plunge back into adultery."

5. Do you see your need for a purified heart? In light of this chapter, what are some of the things (i.e., beliefs, attitudes, desires, activities, etc.) that God is putting His finger on in your life right now that need to be purified?

6. Read Mark 7:20-23 and Galatians 5:16-23. These passages contrast the type of fruit that is manifested in a person's life who is guided by the flesh with the fruit produced by the Holy Spirit—you could also say the fruit of an impure

heart versus the fruit of a pure heart. Which list in Galatians best describes the fruit in your life? Explain your answer.

7. Search your heart and your mind as to what is going on when you and your spouse are being intimate. Are you seeking to just receive pleasure or to give it?

8. According to the author, "The marriage bed is made _____ when the heart of each spouse is made _____."

9. For a more detailed look at sexual intimacy in a Christian marriage you may want to read the book *Intended for Pleasure*, by Dr. Ed Wheat.

1. What is the crowning glory of a life that has been truly conquered by the Holy Spirit?

2. In your own words, explain the two types of peace.

3. Write out the quote from Martyn Lloyd-Jones.

4. Considering the quote from Martyn Lloyd-Jones, are you willing to be a peacemaker in your home and marriage? What will it take? Are there specific changes you need to make in order to become a peacemaker?

5. Generally speaking, do your words promote peace or dissension in your marriage? Explain your answer.

6. Jesus said, "For out of the abundance of the heart the mouth speaks." (Matthew 12:24b) Complete the assignment on "Taming the Tongue" (see Appendix K).

7. Develop a plan and begin to implement the "Conference Table" with your spouse weekly (see Appendix L).

8. Complete Part C of the Sermon on the Mount assignment (see Appendix D).

$\mathscr{A}$PPENDICES

APPENDIX A

RATE YOUR MARRIAGE

This test is designed to evaluate how you are doing in your marriage relationship and to spot problem areas so that you may work on correcting them. The test will be most beneficial if husband and wife both take it and then sit down and discuss their respective answers to each question. Seek to understand clearly the other person's reasons for answering each question as he/she did. If your answers pinpoint some difficulties, focus on how you could resolve the problem. Don't just attack or blame the other person.

Remember, God does have a solution to every problem if you will handle your problems and seek to solve them in a biblical way.

Rating Scale: never = 0; seldom = 1; sometimes = 2; frequently = 3; always = 4.

Write the number that describes what you judge to be true of your marriage in the box preceding each question.

1. Does the fact that Jesus Christ is Lord manifest itself in practical ways in your marriage?
2. Do you use the Bible to determine your convictions, decisions and practices in life in general and marriage in particular?
3. Do you and your spouse study the Bible, pray, worship God and seek to serve God together?
4. Do you and your spouse seek to please one another?
5. Do you ask for forgiveness when you have done something wrong?

6. Do you allow your mate to disagree with you or make a mistake without becoming nasty or punishing him/her?

7. Do you focus on the things you appreciate about your mate and express appreciation in tangible ways?

8. Do you communicate with one another on a daily basis?

9. Do you express your opinions, ideas, plans, aspirations, fears, feelings, likes, dislikes, views, problems, joys, frustrations, annoyances to each other?

10. Do you and your mate understand each other when you try to express yourselves?

11. Do you do many different things together and enjoy being with each other? Are you involved in common projects?

12. Do you show love in many practical and tangible ways?

13. Do you still court one another by occasional gifts, unexpected attention, etc.?

14. Is your conversation pleasant and friendly?

15. Do you pray for one another, support and seek to encourage one another?

16. Can you discuss differing viewpoints on values, priorities, religious convictions, politics, etc., without becoming irritated or upset?

17. Do you anticipate sexual relations with your partner?

18. Are your sexual desires compatible?

19. Do you freely discuss your sexual desires with your mate?

20. Do you agree about the way money should be spent?

21. Do you think your spouse is as concerned about your views about the way money should be spent as he/she is about his/her own?

22. Do you agree on how to bring up your children?

23. Do your children know that it is foolish to try to play one of you against the other; that if Dad says "no," Mother will agree, etc.?

24. Do you refuse to lie to your spouse; are you building your relationship on speaking the truth? Can your spouse put full confidence in whatever you say, knowing that you really mean what you say?

☐ 25. Do you have a good relationship with your in-laws? Do you appreciate them?

☐ 26. Do you really respect your spouse?

☐ 27. Are you glad to introduce your spouse to friends and associates?

☐ 28. Do you control yourself when you are moody so that you do not disrupt your family and inflict your moodiness on others?

☐ 29. Do you seek to change your specific habits that may cause discomfort or displeasure to your spouse?

☐ 30. Do you make your relationship with your spouse a priority matter?

☐ 31. Do you treat your mate with respect and dignity?

☐ 32. Do you accept corrective criticisms graciously?

☐ 33. Do you agree concerning the roles and responsibilities of the husband and wife?

☐ 34. Are you willing to face, discuss, and look for scriptural solutions to problems without blowing up or attacking the other person or dissolving into tears?

☐ 35. Do you maintain your own spiritual life through Bible study, prayer, regular church attendance, and fellowship with God's people?

☐ **TOTAL**

A perfect score for this test would be 140, and this, of course, is the ideal toward which every couple should strive.

Marriages that score 70-94 reveal the need for improvement.

Marriages that score 69 or below are in need of great improvement.

To make this test accurate and, consequently, of maximum value, you ought to be able to support the way you scored each question with specific examples or reasons from your own experience. If you cannot support your score with evidence, your score is suspect.

(Adapted from Edward E. Healy, *The Abiding Word Online*, "Biblical Principles for Christian Growth Online Bible Study")

APPENDIX B

RESTORING COVENANT

This covenant is between you and your spouse and is to be signed by another couple, your pastor or a biblical counselor who will walk alongside you as you seek to live out the principles in this book. It is a 'best practice' to be vulnerable with them as to progress and the status of your marriage. Please complete this covenant with sincerity of heart.

1. *WE COVENANT*...to build our marriage on the principles of Scripture alone.

2. *WE COVENANT*...to allow God to work in our hearts, to dissect us, to show us our sin, to convict us, to change us, to teach us, and to lead us into the truth.

3. *WE COVENANT*...to practice self-denial and to consider the other more important than our self.

4. *WE COVENANT*...to persevere through difficulty, disagreement, fatigue, illness, and any other circumstance that the Almighty allows into our lives for our sanctification.

5. *WE COVENANT*...to pray for God to bring our marriage more and more into His purpose, which is to imitate Christ's relationship to His church as we practice these things faithfully.

6. *WE COVENANT*...to reaffirm our original marital vows and reclaim those under God, despite past failures.

7. *WE COVENANT*...to put off unforgiveness, bitterness, resentment, irresponsibility, vengeance, and all other things contrary to the Word of God.

8. *WE COVENANT*...to put on the fruits of the Spirit toward one another.

9. *WE COVENANT*...to a walk of repentance toward one another in our lives and our marriage.

SIGNED: Husband: _____

Wife: _____

Witness: _____

Witness: _____

Appendix C

"Log" List

"Why do you look at the speck that is in your brother's eye, but do not notice the log that is in your own eye? Or how can you say to your brother, 'Let me take the speck out of your eye,' and behold, the log is in your own eye? You hypocrite, first take the log out of your own eye, and then you will see clearly to take the speck out of your brother's eye." (Matthew 7:3-5 NASB)

1. Get alone with God for an unhurried time of reflection and soul searching. Stop and pray as you begin. Pray according to Psalm 139:23 "Search me, O God, and know my heart; test me and know my anxious thoughts. See if there is any offensive way in me…" Ask God to clearly reveal to you ways that you have wronged your spouse.

2. Get a blank sheet of paper and begin to 'brainstorm.' Make a full list of all the things that you have done and are doing wrong in your marriage. Be honest and specific. We sin against each other in specific, concrete ways, and we need to confess the sin in specific, concrete ways. Try not to be vague or to over-generalize things. The list should be as comprehensive as possible. You should try to have at least 30-50 items listed. Consider ways that you are 'blowing up' your mate's sin and making a big deal of it. Then consider ways that you have been guilty of minimizing your own sins.

3. Privately confess each of the items as sins, and repent before God.

4. Pick a place and time when you can meet together with your spouse. The place should provide an atmosphere in which free and uninterrupted discussion may occur (i.e., make sure the kids are in bed, or get a sitter and go to a hotel for an overnight). The time should be set and kept. Come together with your own list in hand. Begin the meeting by reading Ephesians 4:17-32 and I Corinthians 13:1-8. Try to conduct your meeting together and all of your life according to the principles laid down in these verses.

5. Pray together and ask God's Spirit to meet with you and bring healing. Pray in the name of Jesus that Satan and his powers of darkness would have no place in your hearts or home at this time.

6. Be ready to speak the truth in love (Ephesians 4:15). Do not argue, defend yourself, raise your voice, interrupt, or lose your cool. This meeting is to be a place of healing and reconciliation, not a time to attack, malign, get revenge, or argue. It is a time to uncover and solve problems, not compound them. Do not discuss or debate the validity of the other person's judgment. LISTEN to your spouse. Bite your tongue. Be humble.

    If it becomes obvious at some point that you cannot continue in a godly, productive manner, the meeting should be suspended for an hour or two or until another time. But DO NOT DELAY indefinitely. Satan does not want you to have this meeting! Press on.

    During the interim, force yourself to see things from the other person's point of view. Sit where she/he sits. Think as he/she thinks. Then come back together and proceed.

7. Ready? As the spiritual leader, the husband should begin by confessing his sins and failures to his wife. Be very careful to read each item listed on your *Log List* and say: "I sinned against you", or "I failed you as a husband when I…", or "by not…" "Will you please forgive me?" The wife should respond, "I forgive you." Then move to the next item.

    After the husband has completed going through his list and confessing his sins, the wife should do the same with her list. If you prefer, you can both go through your lists at the same time, alternating back and forth one item at a time… the husband can confess one, then the wife, and so on.

    Having received forgiveness, seek to rectify any wrongs immediately whenever that is possible. Where the change involves the development of a new relationship built on a new, biblical pattern of life, discuss your proposal with your partner and request his/her help in building these new patterns and this new relationship throughout the days ahead.

8. Close in prayer together.

(Adapted from Jay Adams, *Christian Living in the Home*, P&R Publishing, 1972, p. 139-141.)

APPENDIX D

SERMON ON THE MOUNT ASSIGNMENT

Jesus' Sermon on the Mount (Matthew 5-7) clearly reveals the essential elements for personal revival. If you will live in light of these truths, you can experience daily, continuous revival. Failing to heed Christ's words will lead to fruitlessness and despair. So, please take this assignment very seriously and EXPECT the words of Jesus to effect you deeply and to change your heart!

Part A

Answer all 49 questions below. Be very honest with the Lord and with yourself.

YES NO

☐ ☐ 1. Do I have a genuine poverty of spirit? Do I recognize my own inability and the critical need for God in my life? (5:3)

☐ ☐ 2. Do I mourn over my sin? When I sin, is there a godly sorrow that leads to repentance without regret? (5:4; II Cor. 7:10)

☐ ☐ 3. Am I meek? Am I willing to be governed by God alone? Is the quality of brokenness clearly visible in my life? (5:5)

☐ ☐ 4. Am I hungry and thirsty for rightness in every realm of my life? With God? With others? In every situation, circumstance, decision? (5:6)

☐ ☐ 5. Am I merciful toward others? Do I exhibit a spirit of forgiveness? (5:7)

☐ ☐ 6. Am I pure in heart? Are my motives pure? Have I laid down other allegiances and affections that I have cherished more than Jesus? Do I have a single-minded devotion to Jesus Christ? (5:8; II Cor. 11:3)

☐ ☐ 7. Do I seek to be at peace with all men without compromising my convictions? Do I make peace when it is within my power to do so? (5:9; Rom. 12:18)

☐ ☐ 8. Am I standing so visibly for Christ that I am in opposition to the world, the flesh, and the devil and, because of that, suffering persecution? Do I rejoice when men revile me and say all kinds of evil against me falsely for Christ's sake? (5:10-12)

YES   NO

☐   ☐   9. Does my life create a hunger and thirst for God in the lives of others? Am I being used of God now to preserve and maintain the truth? (5:13)

☐   ☐   10. Does my life illuminate the truth about God and man before others? Do people see my good works (the fruit of the Spirit) and glorify God? (5:14-16; Gal. 5:22-23)

☐   ☐   11. Are there any commandments, even the smallest ones, which I do not regard as binding on my life? Am I teaching others to do the same either by expression or example? (5:17-19; Deut. 8:3b)

☐   ☐   12. Is my righteousness merely external, like that of the Pharisees, instead of coming from my heart? (5:20; 22:36-38)

☐   ☐   13. Am I angry with my brothers? Am I guilty of calling others names, criticizing others, or wrongly accusing others? (5:21-22)

☐   ☐   14. Is there anyone, anywhere, who has something against me whom I have not approached to seek reconciliation? (5:23-24)

☐   ☐   15. Am I overcoming lust daily? Are my eyes on Christ alone as my source of satisfaction? Do I have a single-minded devotion in my marriage to my spouse? (5:27-32)

☐   ☐   16. Do I make oaths? Do I feel the necessity to make up for a lack of integrity by assuring people that what I'm saying is really true? Do I ever fail to speak with honesty and integrity? Do I exaggerate or "stretch the truth"? (5:34-37)

☐   ☐   17. Am I taking revenge on anyone by my words or actions? Even subtly? Am I failing to love them aggressively, merely tolerating them? (5:38-39)

☐   ☐   18. Am I giving to my enemies, loving them, praying for them, greeting them? (5:40-47)

☐   ☐   19. Am I seeking to be "perfect" or complete in every realm of my life even as my heavenly Father is perfect? (5:48)

☐   ☐   20. Am I practicing my righteousness before men? Am I anxious to let people know, one way or another, how spiritual I am—what religious activities I'm involved in? (6:1)

☐   ☐   21. When I give, do I make sure others know about it? Am I secretly pleased when they discover it? (6:2-4)

YES NO

☐ ☐ 22. When I pray, am I anxious to impress others? Do I love to pray publicly so that others can hear me and be impressed? (6:5)

☐ ☐ 23. When I pray, do I go into the inner room of my heart and shut the door? Do I pray to my Father? Am I experiencing genuine communion and intimacy with Him? (6:6)

☐ ☐ 24. Do I use meaningless repetitions in prayer? Do I secretly think I can impress God with my many words, or long moments spent in prayer? Am I resting and depending on my own efforts and abilities to gain God's attention rather than the merits of Christ alone? (6:7)

☐ ☐ 25. Am I acknowledging and praising God in prayer? Am I hallowing His Name? Am I praying for His honor and glory? Do my requests reflect a desire for His glory, not just a desire for my own comfort, pleasure, and good will? (6:9)

☐ ☐ 26. Am I aggressively praying for God's kingdom to be established? (6:10)

☐ ☐ 27. Am I praying for God's will to be done—not merely interested in my selfish desires being granted? (6:10)

☐ ☐ 28. Am I depending upon Christ alone as the source of my every need—my daily bread? Do I come to Him with every need of life? (6:11)

☐ ☐ 29. Am I consistently dealing with sin in my life, seeking God's cleansing and forgiveness? (6:12)

☐ ☐ 30. Am I praying for and depending on God's protection from temptation and deliverance from evil? (6:13)

☐ ☐ 31. Is there anyone who has sinned against me, offended me, or harmed me in any way that I have not truly and fully forgiven? (6:14-15)

☐ ☐ 32. Am I fasting? Am I abstaining from worldly issues that cloud my spiritual vision? Have I surrendered every material thing in my life that I felt I cannot do without, or that I couldn't or wouldn't give up on a moment's notice? (6:16)

☐ ☐ 33. When I fast, am I anxious for others to know? (6:16-18)

☐ ☐ 34. Do I have an over-attention to storing up material wealth? Do I own a lot of unnecessary things? Are material possessions seen as "treasures" to me? (6:19)

YES   NO

35. Am I so investing my life and resources that I am laying up treasures and rewards in heaven? (6:20-21)

36. Do I have anything that is a master to me other than the Lord Jesus Christ? Am I holding on to anything in my life that is causing me in some way to treat Christ and the things of God lightly? Causing me to despise Christ or give Him less than His rightful place? (6:24)

37. Am I worrying about material things? About what I will eat or drink or wear? Am I worried unduly about my physical appearance? Am I exhibiting a lack of faith by worrying about anything material? (6:25-31)

38. Am I seeking first of all His kingdom and His righteousness in everything? Am I investing my life and time in eternal, kingdom business (i.e., the Word of God and the lives of others)? (6:33)

39. Am I worrying about the future on any level—worrying about myself, my family, my job, my income, my physical comfort? (6:34)

40. Am I judging others in a critical, condemning, or hypocritical way? (7:1-2)

41. Am I more concerned about changing others than I am about dealing with my own spiritual deficiencies? (7:3-4)

42. Do I try to correct others without first humbly correcting myself? (7:5)

43. Am I asking, seeking, and knocking before the Lord? Am I consistently and continually looking to Him with dependency and expectation, realizing that "He is, and that He is a rewarder of them that seek Him"? (7:7-11; Heb. 11:6)

44. Am I treating others as I would desire them to treat me? Do I give others as much honor, respect, understanding, and attention as I give myself? (7:12)

45. Have I entered the narrow gate that leads to true eternal life? (7:13-14)

46. Am I wary of false prophets? Do I have such a relationship with God and His Word that I am sensitive and discerning regarding that which is really true and that which is false—not naive and gullible regarding spiritual deception? (7:15-20)

YES   NO

☐   ☐   47. Am I trusting in my religious activities to make me right with
            God? Am I vainly believing that external righteousness alone
            will make me right before God? (7:21-23)

☐   ☐   48. Am I consistently in a position to hear the Word of God?
            Am I listening intently to what God is trying to say to me,
            not merely paying casual attention? (7:24)

☐   ☐   49. Am I actively and immediately obeying God as He speaks
            to my heart through His Word? Is my life being built upon
            God's Word through instant obedience to Him? (7:24-27)

Part B

In a journal (or small composition book), write out a short prayer each day considering your answers to two questions at a time. For example, let's say you answer "No" to questions 1-4. In your composition book, you will use the following format:

Day One, Questions 1 & 2:

Dear Lord, I acknowledge to You that I am not very poor in spirit and don't always see my desperate need. I don't really mourn over my sin as I ought to. I beg you to grant me poverty of spirit by bringing me down and into the reality of my great need for You. I thank You that it is your will for me to be poor in spirit and will be faithful to meet my need as You see fit to do so. I am trusting You to change my heart and make me the man/woman of God You want me to be. In Your name I pray. AMEN.

Day Two, Questions 3 & 4:

Dear Lord, I am not meek and I really don't have a hunger and thirst for righteousness. But I do want to be meek and I do want a hunger for the things of God. Please change me, Lord. Deliver me from the prison of SELF. I thank You that You have allowed my present difficulties in order to do a deep work in my heart and I thank You that Your words are doing just that. AMEN.

Part C

For the next month, incorporate Matthew 5-7 into your daily Bible study. Read through these chapters a few times (at least 3 times) to start with. Then begin studying each chapter, verse by verse, and ask the Lord to give you understanding.

(Adapted from Bill Elliff, "Praying Through the Sermon on the Mount" *Life Action Revival Ministries*, www.lifeaction.org, ©1992)

APPENDIX E

BIBLICAL ROLES OF THE HUSBAND AND WIFE

The Biblical Role of the Husband

- He is to leave his parents and cleave to his wife. (Genesis 2:18-25)
- The husband is to be God-centered and others-oriented. (Matthew 6:33; 22:37-40)
- The husband is to serve as Christ. (Matthew 20:28; Mark 10:43-44; Philippians 2:7)
- The husband is not to lord his authority over his wife. (Ephesians 5:25; I Peter 3:7)
- The husband is to learn how to walk in the fear the Lord. (Psalm 128:1-2)
- The husband is to submit to his wife by putting aside his own interest in order to care for his wife. (Ephesians 5:21)
- Ephesians 5:25-33 describes the role of the husband and his love for his wife:
  a) It is a sacrificial love. (v. 25)
  b) It is a cleansing love. (v. 26)
  c) It is a nourishing love. (v. 29)
  d) It is a caring love. (v. 29)

The Biblical Role of the Wife

- The wife is to leave her parents and cleave to her husband. (Genesis 2:18-25)
- The wife is to be God-centered and others-oriented. (Matthew 6:33; 22:37-40)
- The wife is to serve as Christ. (Matthew 20:28; Mark 10:43-44; Philippians 2:7)
- The wife is to submit to her husband as unto the Lord. (Ephesians 5:22-24)
- The wife is to respect her husband's leadership and his decisions. (Ephesians 5:33)
- The wife is to care for her household. (Proverbs 31)
- The wife is to walk in the fear of the Lord. (Proverbs 31:30)
- The wife is to be a fruitful vine. (Galatians 5:22-23; I Peter 3:1-5; John 15:1,5)
- The wife is to be a complementary helper to her husband. (Genesis 2:18)

APPENDIX F

DEVELOPING A DEVOTIONAL TIME

Hopefully you're fully convinced by now that a prayer life is essential for your spiritual vitality. However, if you want to build Bible reading and prayer into your life as consistent, daily practices, you need to have a blueprint. You'll have to draw up your own individually tailored plan, but here are some helpful tips to ensure success.

1. Decide when you will pray.

Set aside a block of time everyday, preferably in the morning, when you will pray. E.M. Bounds said, "If God is not the first in our thoughts and efforts in the morning, He will be last, during the day." If you don't feel like you have the time, write out a schedule of what you do with your time throughout the day. Review this schedule and make changes so you will have time. Nothing can be more important than setting time aside for God.

2. Have a place to pray.

Find a place where you can be alone with God. Find a secret place where lovers can meet to share time alone with one another. God will wait for you there, anticipating His time with you.

3. Decide what you will do with your time there.

You can spend some time just worshiping Him. You can use something like Psalm 103 or any number of Psalms to help you. Worship should always be right on the tip of our tongue as we consider who God is and the love He has manifested toward us in Jesus Christ. Spend time repenting of where you have fallen short in your marriage vows and in your personal walk. Pray for the needs of others, especially your spouse. Have some time in the Word, reading it, studying it, meditating on it, and praying over it.

4. Do it everyday!

If you will be consistent, you will begin to develop a habit and will begin to look forward to your time alone with God.

5. *As you grow, you will want to increase the length of time.*

Fifteen minutes won't cut it. Sometimes it can take 15 minutes just to rein in our mind and subdue our flesh. If you want to benefit from your time with God, it has to be quality time that isn't rushed.

6. *Spend time in prayer together as a couple.*

When a couple prays together, it cultivates vulnerability with one another and builds strength into the relationship. That said, wives should refrain from putting an unnecessary burden on their husband to pray with them every day. (If you both feel that is desirable, that's fine.) But couples should at least set aside time once during the week when they will be able to come together and pray. The most important thing is that a couple takes the time to pray together. It will produce bonding and foster the closeness that is needed to restore and maintain the health of your marriage.

APPENDIX G

THE LOVE TEST

God's love has many attributes and we have to look to His Word to understand what they are. Take a simple passage like I Corinthians 13:4-8. Through this one passage we can start changing the way we see and act toward our spouse. Prayerfully consider each of the questions below and allow the Holy Spirit to reveal your heart. After making an honest evaluation, write down areas where change is needed and formulate a plan to implement the truths you've learned, realizing of course that this is a life long process.

Love suffers long:

Am I patient with my spouse? In my day to day dealings with him/her, do I exhibit the longsuffering God has shown toward me? Am I willing to bear his/her faults as my own, and pray for him/her instead of hurting and injuring him/her by my short-suffering?

Love is kind:

Am I kind in the way I speak to my spouse? Is my speech edifying, or harsh and cutting? If we truly love our spouse we will be kind to him/her and seek to do good to him/her instead of behaving harshly or desiring revenge. Kindness will reveal itself in the way we act toward one another. Am I polite toward my spouse? If we are truly under the influence of God's love, it will show in our politeness and compassion toward one another.

Love does not envy:

Do I rejoice for my spouse when he/she is successful and being blessed by God, or do I get resentful and wish I could get something for myself? Love always rejoices to see the other happy and blessed by God.

Love does not parade itself:

Am I constantly throwing up in my spouse's face what I am doing right and promoting myself to him/her? Love does its alms in secret and seeks to promote the other, not self.

Love is not puffed up:

Am I full of pride, and do I consider myself more important than my spouse? A person, who is puffed up, makes themselves extremely important and others less important. For example, do I love to hear myself talk, yet don't listen when my spouse talks? Love seeks to make the other more important.

Love does not behave rudely:

In other words, a person who loves is nice. Do I respect my spouse and treat him/her accordingly? Are there things I could change that offend my spouse? Love seeks to avoid anything that would offend and not promote the well-being of your spouse.

Love does not seek its own:

Love is not selfish. Do things tend to revolve around my happiness and satisfaction, or am I focused on blessing and meeting the needs of my spouse? Are there things I do or expect from my spouse that revolve around getting what I want, rather than pleasing God and putting his/her needs before my own?

Love is not provoked:

How do I respond when my spouse does something I don't like? Do I get angry and allow myself to vent my irritation, or do I choose at that moment to do something different from the heart? A person, who is yielding to God's love, looks at things through His eyes. He or she learns to subdue personal feelings and to do what pleases God, which most of the time will simply be to pray for the other person. Jesus made it clear that we are to pray for a person that wrongs us in anyway. If you are willing to do that, you will not be easily provoked.

Love thinks no evil:

Your mind can be your worst enemy. Where does my mind go with regard to my spouse? Do I jump to conclusions and believe the worst about him/her? Love believes the best about someone's motives and intentions. Do I keep a record of his/her faults and evils, instead of thinking on the good things about him/her? Love discards any wrong that has been done in the past and thinks on what is best for the future.

Love does not rejoice in iniquity, but in the truth:

Do I secretly take pleasure when my spouse has something exposed that he/she has done wrong? Love doesn't rejoice in the sins of others, but rejoices in the truth. Do I rejoice that God can now cleanse that fault? Do I rejoice because he/she is forgiven? Do I rejoice in the good that will come out of it for him/her? Love rejoices in the truth.

Love bears all things:

Do I just try to put up with my spouse, or do I bear him/her as Jesus bore me? Jesus overlooks our imperfections and bears us to God in order to relieve us of these shortcomings. Do I look at my spouse with a microscope looking for any imperfection, or do I tend to overlook them and pray for him/her instead?

Love believes all things:

Do I believe the best about my spouse? Do I hold onto what God promised He could do for him/her by faith?

Love hopes all things:

Do I believe and trust that God can do what is needed for my spouse, despite what I may see? Love always hopes in God and puts the other person in His merciful hands. Do I ever tell my spouse, "You'll never change?"

Love endures all things:

Do I murmur and complain about the burden of my spouse and my situation, or do I patiently bear up under it? Do I see my spouse and my situation as a direct agent of God's providence in my life? Am I willing to embrace whatever God allows through my marriage to bring about His good and His purpose through it?

Love never fails:

Is love the most important thing I am seeking to live out in my marriage? Love will abide forever. Everything else will cease to exist, but God's love will endure forever. It should be our highest goal toward one another as His followers. Each spouse should be seeking that which has enduring and everlasting value.

"Love one another as I have loved you." (John 13:34)

APPENDIX H

A PRAYER FOR CHRISTIAN LOVE

If you don't see much of God's love in your heart, don't fret. He knows how to give you His love as you turn to Him and believe Him to help you. God doesn't want us to despair, but to believe Him for what seems impossible to us. Here is an old Puritan prayer that can help you believe God to give you the Christian love you do not yet possess.

"Lord I thank You that You love the loveless.

It is Your will that I love You with my whole heart,

soul, mind, and strength, and that I also love my neighbor as myself.

Yet I see that in myself I am not sufficient to do this, because by nature

there is not a drop of pure agape love in my soul. Every one of my affections

is not always turned toward You, and at times I am still a slave to my carnal

lusts. I see that I cannot love You, as lovely as You are, until I am utterly set free

from my sinful self. By Your Grace I am free and able to serve You, because

I believe You are my God through Christ who shed His blood for me.

Through Him I am redeemed, and my sins are forgiven.

May Your Spirit draw me nearer to You and

to Your ways. You alone are the end to all means,

and if I am not led to You, I will go away empty. Direct all of my

ways by Your word, and make it the joy of my heart, that I may have

sweet fellowship with You. Help me to grow in Your love and to manifest

it to others. Make me more like Jesus in my thoughts and in my actions,

so Your light can shine before men. Humble me more, make me meek

and lowly at heart, and help me always to honor and to

please You in all things."

[*The Valley of Vision, A Collection of Puritan Prayers and Devotions*, Arthur G. Bennett, editor (Carlisle, PA: Banner of Truth, 2003.]

APPENDIX I

THE "ONE ANOTHER" PASSAGES

Bible passages essential for us to understand and develop healthy relationships by knowing we are called to *One Another*.

- *Love* one another: John 13:34-35; 15:12, 17; Romans 12:10; 13:8; I Thessalonians 3:12; 4:9; II Thessalonians 1:3; I Peter 1:22; I John 3:11, 3:23; 4:7, 11-12; II John 1: 5

- *Serve* one another: Galatians 5:13; Philippians 2:3-4; I Peter 4:9-10

- *Accept* one another: Romans 15:7; Ephesians 4:2

- *Strengthen* one another: Romans 14:19

- *Help* one another: Hebrews 3:13; 10:24

- *Encourage* one another: Romans 14:19; 15:14; Colossians 3:16; I Thessalonians 5:11; Hebrews 3:13; 10:24-25

- *Care for* one another: I Corinthians 12:25; Galatians 6:2

- *Forgive* one another: Ephesians 4:32; Colossians 3:13

- *Submit to* one another: Ephesians 5:21; I Peter 5:5

- *Commit to* one another: I John 3:16

- *Build trust with* one another: I John 1:7

- *Be devoted to* one another: Romans 12:10

- *Be patient with* one another: Ephesians 4:2; Colossians 3:13

- *Be interested in* one another: Philippians 2:4

- *Be accountable to* one another: Ephesians 5:21

- *Confess to* one another: James 5:16

- *Live in harmony with* one another: Romans 12:16

- *Do not be conceited to* one another: Romans 13:8

- *Do not pass judgment on* one another: Romans 14:13; 15:7

- *Do not slander* one another: James 4:11

- **Instruct** *one another:* Romans 16:16
- **Greet** *one another:* Romans 16:16; I Corinthians 1:10;
  II Corinthians 13:12
- **Admonish** *one another:* Romans 5:14; Colossians 3:16
- **Spur** *one another* **on toward love and good deeds**:
  Hebrews 10:24
- **Meet with** *one another:* Hebrews 10:25
- **Agree with** *one another:* I Corinthians 16:20
- **Be concerned for** *one another:* Hebrews 10:24
- **Be humble to** *one another* **in love**: Ephesians 4:2
- **Be compassionate to** *one another:* Ephesians 4:32
- **Do not be consumed by** *one another:* Galatians 5:14-15
- **Do not anger** *one another:* Galatians 5:26
- **Do not lie to** *one another:* Colossians 3:9
- **Do not grumble to** *one another:* James 5:9
- **Give preference to** *one another:* Romans 12:10
- **Be at peace with** *one another:* Romans 12:18
- **Sing to** *one another:* Ephesians 5:19
- **Be of the same mind to** *one another:* Romans 12:16; 15:5
- **Comfort** *one another:* I Thessalonians 4:18; 5:11
- **Be kind to** *one another:* Ephesians 4:32
- **Live in peace with** *one another:* I Thessalonians 5:13
- **Carry** *one another's* **burdens**: Galatians 6:2

(Adapted from *Into Thy Word Ministries*, www.intothyword.org, 2000)

APPENDIX J

PRAYER OF MERCY

One of the particular benefits of this prayer outline is its ability to let God change your heart toward the one you are praying for. Bear in mind that the words of this prayer are not meant to be memorized and repeated as a rigid script. Rather, as you gain familiarity with this outline, each bullet point should eventually become only a theme or heading to guide your prayer.

• Lord, I thank you for _____. Thank you for saving her/him. Thank you for what you have done and are doing in her/his life. (Ephesians 1:16; Philippians 4:6; Colossians 1:3; I Thessalonians 1:2; 3:9; 5:18; II Thessalonians 2:13)

• Make _____ to know Jesus. Help her/him to increase in the knowledge of God. Destroy speculations and every lofty thing raised up against the knowledge of God and help her/him to bring every thought captive to the obedience of Christ. (John 17:3; II Corinthians 10:5; Colossians 1:10; 2:3; 3:10)

• Make _____ poor in spirit. Bring her/him down, but please do it gently. Help her/him to see their neediness. Help her/him to see her/himself in light of you. Put her/him in their rightful place, Lord. (Psalm 51:17; Matthew 5:3; Proverbs 29:23; Isaiah 66:2; I Peter 5:5)

• Fill _____ with Your Holy Spirit. (Luke 11:13; Acts 4:31; I Corinthians 6:19)

• Life* _____. Life her/him according to Your lovingkindness. Pour out Your life-giving mercies into her/his soul. (Psalm 80:18; Psalm 119:25, 37, 50, 88, 107, 149, 154, 156, 159; Psalm 143:11; Romans 8:11)

• Bless _____. Lord bless her/him in everything she/he touches. Bless her/him spiritually, physically and financially. Bless her/his loved ones. Do for her/him, Lord, instead of me. (Genesis 12:1-3; Proverbs 10:22; Matthew 5:44, Romans 12:14, 20; I Peter 2:23; 3:9)

• Mercy _____. Flood her/him with need filling mercies. Pour them out in super abundance. Find and meet every need in her/his life as You see it Lord. As you have mercied me, so mercy her or him. (Psalm 86:5; Hosea 6:6; Matthew 9:13; II Corinthians 1:3)

(Adapted from Rex Andrews, *What the Bible Teaches About Mercy*, Zion Faith Homes, 1985.)

---

* The word *Life* is used here as a verb, in order to coincide with the biblical use of the Hebrew word *chayah,* which is more commonly translated as *revive* or *quicken* (KJV), but carries the deeper meaning of imparting spiritual life to someone.

APPENDIX K

TAMING THE TONGUE

1. Each day, look up one of the following chapters from Proverbs and write out any verses you find relating to our speech: Proverbs 10, 12, 15, 17 & 18. Meditate on these verses throughout the day.

2. Read James 3:1-13 and then list all the things these verses said about our tongue.

3. Read Romans 3:10-18 and then list what Paul had to say about the tongue in these verses.

4. According to Ephesians 4:29-31, what do we do to the Holy Spirit when we allow any ungodly words to come out of our mouths?

5. Read Matthew 12:36-37.
   a) Are we going to be held accountable before God for what we say?
   b) According to Jesus, how will we be condemned?
   c) How will we be justified?

6. God listens to everything we say:
   - About Him
   - About other people
   - And what we tell other people

   With this in mind, make Psalm 19:12-14 a prayer every day this week. (Remember you can always repent if you blow it.)

7. What kind of advice does Scripture give us in James 1:19-20? Why?

8. According to Ecclesiastes 5:2-6 what can cause us to sin? How can we be wise?

9. In Galatians 5:13-15, what danger are we in if we are not walking in love toward others and if we have no control over our tongue?

10. What are some stumbling blocks in your words that affect your relationship with God? With others?

11. Based on Colossians 4:6, what should our conduct be in this area? What do the terms "grace" and "seasoned with salt" mean to you?

APPENDIX L

THE CONFERENCE TABLE

Purposes & Procedures

The Conference Table is a place to confer, not argue or cast blame upon each other. Participants should agree in advance upon the place where the daily conference may be held without interruption; agree also on how long the conference should last and stick to the time established. Choose a table, preferably one that is not used frequently for other purposes. Hold all conferences there. If problems arise elsewhere throughout the day, whenever possible wait until you reach home to discuss them at the conference table.

Each Conference Table should begin in prayer. Next, read and review Ephesians 4:17-32 for Biblical communication guidelines.

To begin each meeting, each person takes a turn and shares about themselves and how they have sinfully responded or sinfully handled any problems since the last Conference Table session. If forgiveness needs to be asked, do so. Speak all truth in love. Do not allow any sinful issues to be carried over into the next day. After each person has confessed their own sins and failures, they can then each bring up issues and problems which need to be discussed. As not all problems can be solved in one sitting, you may find it necessary to make up an agenda and schedule the work over a period of time based upon priority.

As problems are brought up and conferring begins, direct all your energies toward defeating the problem, not the other person. Your goal is to reach a Biblical solution, so always have a Bible on the table and use it to the best of your ability. It helps to have a written record of the meeting and the results, steps or goals that are decided upon.

How to Handle Trouble

If any participant clams up or does anything other than confer (discuss) at the table, the other(s) must raise their hand or stand up quietly. This signal must be agreed upon before the conference begins. This signal means, "In my opinion, we have stopped conferring." Whether this person is right or wrong in this judgment does not matter, and should not be discussed at the moment. The person seated should then indicate his/her willingness to confer and invite the other(s) to be seated again.

After ½ hour of conferring, and an impasse is reached rather than a Biblical solution, reschedule the problem again for the next meeting, each promising to pray thoroughly about the problem and their individual ideas, and any wrong motives, etc. If an impasse is still reached, it will then be necessary to contact an outside source – preferably a Pastor, Elder, Deacon or Biblical Counselor. (Proverbs 11:14; 24:6)

Rules

- Husband, as head of the home, calls the conference, is in charge of the meeting, makes sure the meeting ends on time.
- Wife can also call a meeting.
- Wife takes notes of the meeting.
- Begin conference in prayer, read Ephesians 4:17-32 and review rules.
- Allow each participant time for confession and repentance of current issues.
- Discuss problem topics and decide agenda together. Proceed with conference.
- End in prayer.

Conference Table Meeting Record

Date: _____

Begin Time: _____   End Time: _____

Problem(s) to be Discussed:

1.

2.

3.

Outcome/Steps to be Implemented/Goals:

[Adapted from Jay Adams, *The Christian Counselor's Manual* (Grand Rapids, MI: Zondervan Publishing House, 1973) p. 321-326.]

ｴOTES

CHAPTER ONE

1. Meg Flammang, Barna Project, http://www.religioustolerance.org/chr_dira.htm

2 Steve Gallagher, *At the Altar of Sexual Idolatry* (Dry Ridge, KY: Pure Life Ministries, 2007) p. 199.

CHAPTER TWO

1. D. Martyn Lloyd-Jones, *Studies in the Sermon on the Mount* (Grand Rapids, MI: Eerdmans Publishing Co., 1959) p. 42.

2. Albert Barnes, "Matthew: Chapter 4" *Barnes' Notes on the Bible Vol. 12,* as cited in *AGES Digital Library* (Rio, WI: AGES Software, Inc., 2001) p. 121.

3. Georgiana M. Taylor, "Oh, To Be Nothing." http://www.cyberhymnal.org/htm/o/t/b/o2bnothn.htm

4. William Barclay, as quoted in *Inspiring Quotations: Contemporary and Classical* compiled by Albert Wells (Nashville, TN: Thomas Nelson, Inc., 1988).

5. D. Martin Lloyd-Jones, p. 36.

CHAPTER THREE

1. François Fénelon, *The Seeking Heart* (Jacksonville, FL: Seedsowers Christian Books Publishing, 1982) p. 17.

2 Sinclair Ferguson, *The Sermon on The Mount: Kingdom Life in a Fallen World* (Carlisle, PA: The Banner of Truth Trust, 1987) p. 18.

3. D. Martyn Lloyd-Jones, p. 49.

4. Steve Gallagher, *At the Altar of Sexual Idolatry*, p. 201-202.

5. A.W. Tozer, as cited in Warren Wiersbe, *The Best of A.W. Tozer* (Grand Rapids, MI: Baker Publishing House, 1978) p. 61.

CHAPTER FOUR

1. Roy Hession, *The Calvary Road* (Ft. Washington, PA: Christian Literature Crusade, 1990) p. 22.

2. Rex Andrews, *Meditations in the Revelation* (Zion, IL: Zion Faith Homes, 1991) p. 63.

3. Kay Arthur, *A Marriage Without Regrets* (Eugene, OR: Harvest House Publishers, 2000) p. 71, 72.

CHAPTER FIVE

1. C. J. Mahaney, *The Cross-Centered Life* (Sisters, OR: Multnomah Books, 2002) p. 31.

2. D. Martyn Lloyd-Jones, p. 67.

3. Steve Gallagher, *Intoxicated with Babylon* (Dry Ridge: KY: Pure Life Ministries, 1996) p. 67.

4. D. Martyn Lloyd-Jones, p. 65, 66.

5. Martin Luther as quoted in E. M. Bounds, *Power Through Prayer* (New Kensington, PA: Whitaker House, 1982) p. 45.

6. Andrew Murray, *The Inner Life* (New Kensington, PA: Whitaker House, 1985) p. 17, 23.

7. Charles H. Spurgeon, "Faiths Checkbook," *Books for the Ages,* as cited in *AGES Digital Library* (Rio, WI: AGES AGES Digital Software, Inc., 2001) p. 316.

CHAPTER SIX

1. Rex Andrews, *What the Bible Teaches About Mercy*, (Zion, IL: Zion Faith Homes, 1985) p. 2.

2. D. Martyn Lloyd-Jones, p. 81, 82.

CHAPTER SEVEN

1. Gary Thomas, *Sacred Marriage* (Grand Rapids, MI: Zondervan, 2000) p. 13.

2. Joseph Thayer, *Thayer's Greek-English Lexicon of the New Testament* (Peabody, MA: Hendrickson Publishers, Inc., 1981).

3. Rex Andrews, *What the Bible Teaches About Mercy*, p. 197.

4. D. Martyn Lloyd-Jones, p. 94.

5. Kay Arthur, p. 159.

6. Charles Finney, "Blessedness of the Pure in Heart" *The Oberlin Evangelist*, 1858, http://www.gospeltruth.net/1858OE/580901_pure_blessed.htm

CHAPTER EIGHT

1. "Luke: Chapter 11," *The Biblical Illustrator*, as cited in *AGES Digital Library* (Rio, WI: AGES Software, Inc., 2001) p. 54.

2. D. Martyn Lloyd-Jones, p. 102, 105.

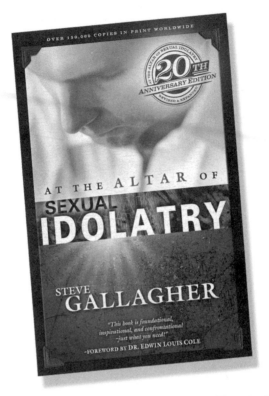

OVER 150,000 COPIES IN PRINT WORLDWIDE

20TH ANNIVERSARY EDITION
REVISED & EXPANDED

AT THE ALTAR OF
SEXUAL
IDOLATRY

STEVE
GALLAGHER

"This book is foundational,
inspirational, and confrontational
—just what you need!"
—FOREWORD BY DR. EDWIN LOUIS COLE

THE MOST COMPREHENSIVE BOOK ON SEXUAL SIN AVAILABLE TODAY!

Sexual temptation is undeniably the greatest struggle Christian men face. Here's a book that digs deep and has the answers men are looking for—the kind that actually work. While other books deal with the subject superficially, *At the Altar of Sexual Idolatry* goes right to the heart. Put an end to the mystery of lust and maximize God's power in your life with the proven answers that have helped thousands.

WORKBOOK
ALSO AVAILABLE

*Spanish translation
available as well.*

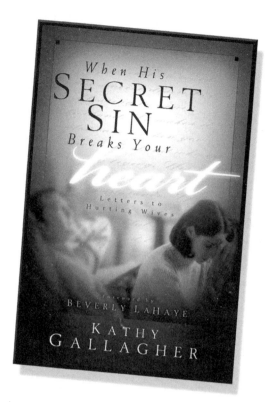

WHERE TO TURN WHEN SEXUAL SIN DEVASTATES A MARRAIGE.

What can be more devastating for a wife than to discover her husband has a secret obsession with pornography and other women? Yet, this is what countless Christian wives face every day. Kathy Gallagher has been there; she understands the pain of rejection, the feelings of hopelessness and the questions that plague a hurting wife. In this collection of letters, Kathy imparts heart-felt encouragement by providing the practical, biblical answers that helped her find healing in the midst of her most trying storm. The 30-day journal offers wives a place to prayerfully reflect and meditate upon Kathy's letters.

CREATE IN ME A PURE HEART

NO LONGER JUST A MAN'S ISSUE! Current statistics reveal that Christian women are becoming involved in pornography and cyber-sex in alarming numbers. *Create in Me a Pure Heart* addresses the unique issues struggling women face and offers the biblical wisdom and sensitive counsel that will lead women to freedom. For over 20 years Steve and Kathy Gallagher have helped Christian men find victory from sexual sin. Now *Create in Me a Pure Heart* extends this liberating legacy to struggling women.

A BIBLICAL GUIDE TO COUNSELING THE SEXUAL ADDICT

A SERIOUS book for Christian Counselors
Christian men scoping pornography…
Adulterous eyes in the pulpit…
Casual sex among singles…
Now, more than ever, the Church needs godly people willing to passionately impart biblical truths to those drowning in the cesspool of sexual idolatry. Tackle the tough issues with this practical guide gleaned from over 20 years of experience!

IRRESISTIBLE TO GOD

Before a person can come into intimate contact with a Holy God, he must first be purged of the hideous cancer of pride that lurks deep within his heart.

"This book is a road map that shows the arduous but rewarding way out of the pit of pride and into the green pastures of humility. Here is the place of blessing and favor with God"—Steve Gallagher

Humility is the key that opens the door into the inner regions of intimacy with God. *Irresistible to God* unfolds the mystery that God is indeed drawn to the one who is crushed in spirit, broken by his sin, and meek before the Lord and others.

INTOXICATED WITH BABYLON

The strength of *Intoxicated With Babylon* is Steve Gallagher's sobering deliverance of the unvarnished truth to a Church rife with sensuality and worldly compromise. In a time when evangelical Christians seem content to be lulled to sleep by the spirit of Antichrist, *Intoxicated With Babylon* sounds a clarion wake-up call in an effort to draw the Body of Christ back to the Cross and holy living. Those with itching ears will find no solace here, but sincere believers will experience deep repentance and a fresh encounter with the Living God.

To Order Visit Our Web Site or Call TOLL FREE 888.PURELIFE

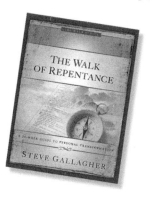
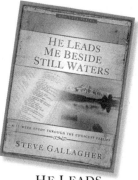
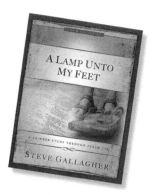

Pure Life Ministries

Pure Life Ministries helps Christian men achieve lasting freedom from sexual sin. The Apostle Paul said, "Walk in the Spirit and you will not fulfill the lust of the flesh." Since 1986, Pure Life Ministries (PLM) has been discipling men into the holiness and purity of heart that comes from a Spirit-controlled life. At the root, illicit sexual behavior is sin and must be treated with spiritual remedies. Our counseling programs and teaching materials are rooted in the biblical principles that, when applied to the believer's daily life, will lead him out of bondage and into freedom in Christ.

Biblical Teaching Materials

Pure Life Ministries offers a full line of books, audio CDs and DVDs specifically designed to give men the tools they need to live in sexual purity.

Residential Care

The most intense and involved counseling PLM offers comes through the **Live-In Program** (6-12 months), in Dry Ridge, Kentucky. The godly and sober atmosphere on our 45-acre campus provokes the hunger for God and deep repentance that destroys the hold of sin in men's lives.

Help At Home

The **Overcomers At Home Program** (OCAH) is available for those who cannot come to Kentucky for the Live-In program. This twelve-week counseling program features weekly counseling sessions and many of the same teachings offered in the Live-In Program.

Care For Wives

Pure Life Ministries also offers help to wives of men in sexual sin. Our wives' counselors have suffered through the trials and storms of such a discovery and can offer a devastated wife a sympathetic ear and the biblical solutions that worked in their lives.

Pure Life Ministries
14 School St. • Dry Ridge • KY • 41035
Office: 859.824.4444 • Orders: 888.293.8714
info@purelifeministries.org
www.purelifeministries.org